cooking with
GRACE

A COOKBOOK FROM **POINT OF GRACE**
WITH JULIE ADKISON

We can hardly believe that we have our own cookbook and are so honored that you would want to own it! Compiling this collection of our favorite recipes has been a labor of love. "Cooking With Grace" is the perfect title and we never really considered another one. Obviously, it is a play on the name of our group, Point Of Grace, but the idea of the actual act of "cooking with grace" struck something deep inside each one of us.

SHELLEY

SHELLEY: I think a lot of times when you are having people into your home you stress about everything being perfect. To me, "cooking with grace" means the exact opposite. People want to enjoy my family and me. It is not about a clean house or a perfectly executed meal. All I can do is cook for enjoyment and with love, but then just let the chips fall where they may. I want to be a good and attentive hostess who listens and laughs with my guests. I always try to extend graciousness and hospitality in the age-old Southern way!

LEIGH

LEIGH: Day after day, year after year, I watched my mother put a healthy meal on the table without hesitation, not realizing at the time how exhausted she must have been from working all day at her job. She poured out her grace each Sunday afternoon with a feast fit for a king. "Grace cooking" continued to be modeled as she shared her cooking with the next generation. Her grandkids love her chocolate pies, turkey and dressing and most of all, her themed birthday cakes. Mom has a few consistent ingredients in each recipe, as well as in her life: 2 Tablespoons of Joy, a pinch of Peace sprinkled with Patience, fresh cloves of Kindness and Goodness and best for last, the overflowing cups of LOVE!

DENISE

DENISE: When I think about "cooking with grace," I think about all of the women I watched shower love over the hurting or needy by cooking. We often joke about how it's overdone, but here in the South, that is the way we do things. Maybe you don't really need the extra food, but in a time of crisis or need it sure is nice to know that someone cares enough to give you some of their time and love. A plate of cookies or a casserole can speak volumes. Some of the sweetest times of conversation come when you sit down and enjoy a meal together. Why do you think the "Last Supper" was so important? Jesus invites us to His banqueting table. Can you imagine the menu? So as you try out some of these recipes, I pray it's a way to share God's goodness and grace with others.

We sincerely hope that you enjoy reading and using this cookbook as much as we enjoyed making it for you. Proverbs 15:15 says that "a cheerful heart has a continual feast." May your heart, as well as your dinner table, be filled with continual feasting!

Love,

Shelley   Leigh   Denise

Point Of Grace

APPETIZERS

SALADS

SOUPS

CASSEROLES

MEATS

SIDE DISHES

MEXICAN

table of CONTENTS

DESSERTS

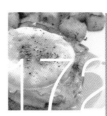

BREAKFAST

SO, YOU'RE HAVING SOME FRIENDS OVER FOR

APPETIZERS

One thing you may have figured out about us is that we're always up for a party! Whether it's the Super Bowl, a baby shower or Bible study, appetizers are a great way to make any occasion more festive. We have even been known to make an entire meal out of them, with a little bit of this and a little taste of that. How can you go wrong?

HOT ONION SOUFFLÉ

from SHELLEY

If people think *I'm* Martha Stewart, it is only because they haven't met my neighbor, Kathy, who lives two doors down. When her dog stole my daughter's favorite stuffed animal, Woof Woof, the next thing I knew a newly washed stuffed animal appeared in my mailbox along with an apology note and three bags of pumpkin chocolate chip muffins. As if that weren't enough, they were neatly packaged in decorative Fall cellophane bags with elaborate ribbon ties! Now who has time to DO that?? (You can find the delicious pumpkin chocolate chip muffin recipe in our breakfast chapter!)

When Kathy and I were just getting to know each other, she and her husband Rick had David and me over for a nice dinner. This is what she served us the first time we visited. Trust me, your friends will love it and will be impressed that the word "soufflé" is in the title!

- 16 oz. bag, frozen, chopped onions (3-4 cups)
- 24 oz. cream cheese, softened
- 2 cups grated Parmesan cheese
- ½ cup mayonnaise
- corn chips or assorted crackers

1. Preheat oven to 350.
2. Thaw onions. Roll them in paper towels, squeezing to remove excess water.
3. Stir together onions, cream cheese, Parmesan cheese and mayonnaise until well combined.
4. Transfer to a shallow 2-quart baking dish.
5. Bake about 15 minutes or until golden brown.
6. Serve with corn chips or assorted crackers

Makes 6 Cups (serves 12-14 people)

This can easily be halved.

Montana (stuffed animal thief), Kathy, Shelley, Caroline and the rescued Woof-Woof.

"MEETBALLS"

from LEIGH

Parties often allow us to "meet" new people. Whether old or new friends, this recipe should do the trick. It is simple, yet hearty. This appetizer will be satisfying and filling for the big boys and delicate enough for the ladies.

Oh, how I love using my Crockpot! Using it gives me my life back. I just plug it in and go. That is all it takes for this appetizer to come to life and, hopefully, you will have a "meeting" to be remembered. I had these at a party Shelley was giving not too long ago and decided to ask her how she made them. When she told me the recipe, I couldn't believe it! Take a look at how easy they are.

- One 2½ lb package of frozen meatballs (I get mine at Costco)
- Two 12 oz. bottles of Heinz Chili Sauce
- One 32 oz. jar grape jelly

1. Pour meatballs into Crockpot.
2. Pour chili sauce and grape jelly in large saucepan.
3. Heat on med-hi for 5-10 minutes, stirring until combined.
4. Pour sauce mixture over meatballs.
5. On high cook about 2½ hours. (On medium cook about 3 hours)

Serves 15-20

a quick POINT

Abbreviations that you will see throughout our cookbook:

T. = Tablespoon
t. = teaspoon
oz. = ounce/ounces
lb. = pound
POG = this is the universally accepted abbreviation for Point Of Grace ☺

MISSISSIPPI SIN DIP

from DENISE

Okay, so our cookbook is NOT low fat, but these recipes sure taste good. This particular dip is very sinful! I guess you have to decide for yourself whether you want to participate or not.

- 24 oz. cream cheese, softened
- ½ cup mayonnaise
- 8 oz. chopped green chiles
- 2 cups cheddar cheese
- 16 oz. sour cream
- 12 oz. deli honey ham, very finely chopped

1. Preheat oven to 350.
2. Mix all ingredients together.
3. Bake for 30 minutes 'til hot and bubbly.
4. Serve with corn chips or any type of cracker you like.

Serves 20+

Price, Spence and Denise...
Hmm, no one ever said "Eat no evil!"

COOKING CLASS #1

CLIPPING FRESH HERBS: You will notice that some of our recipes call for fresh herbs that have been minced, chopped or snipped. The easiest way to do this is to place your fresh herbs in a small, short, wide-mouth glass and use kitchen scissors to cut them by putting blades of scissors right down into the glass. Squeeze scissor handles quickly and firmly. The glass will keep the herbs from flying all over your kitchen. (Kitchen scissors are a must-have! You can just stick them in the dishwasher when you are done.)

TOASTED PECANS

from LEIGH

What about toasted pecans as an appetizer? Have you smelled them while shopping at the mall? Well, I grew up on a pecan orchard. When I was a kid, money was not handed to you. You had to earn it! I spent many fall afternoons picking up pecans on our family's land. My granddaddy Ivester's homestead was on several acres and if you were an Ivester, you knew how to find a pecan worthy of pickin'. This was a serious business for my family. I can remember how excited I would get once I had picked up a whole grocery bag full. (And I am not talkin' no silly plastic bag, it was the BIG brown bags.) They had to be all the way to the top before it would equal 25 "big ones." My sisters and I would always race to see who could fill their bag first. Whoooweee! It was the best feeling! We thought we were so rich!

The Ivester homestead, a pecan pickin' extravaganza

Giving the gift of pecans has become a family tradition. My grandmother and mother still give bags of pecans either cracked, shelled or toasted, as Christmas gifts. They give them to family members, friends, schoolteachers and Sunday school teachers. I have always believed it is a matter of "rank" on the Christmas list whether you receive them cracked, shelled or toasted. Toasted is ALWAYS best! (Shelley and Denise only get them shelled – ha ha – just kidding!)

- 2 cups pecan halves
- 4 T. butter, melted
- 1 T. Worcestershire sauce
- salt to taste

1. Preheat oven to 300.
2. Stir pecans, butter and Worcestershire together.
3. Spread into cookie sheet or baking pan.
4. Bake for approximately 30 minutes, stirring every 10 minutes.
5. Sprinkle with salt while still warm.

(Note: You have to watch, watch, watch those babies. Over-toasted (burnt) nuts are nasty and then I will have wasted all that money I earned picking up all those bags of pecans!)

Serves 6-8

BRUSCHETTA APPETIZER

from SHELLEY

There is nothing I love more than a ripe tomato in the thick of summer! I can eat them just sliced with salt and pepper or on a sandwich made of white bread and a little dab of Miracle Whip. However, my favorite tomato combo of all time (besides salsa, of course!!) is a little tomato with fresh basil. This recipe is the perfect combination of those tastes and your guests will love it!

- 12 slices from baguette loaf of bread
- 2-3 T. butter, softened
- 3 plum tomatoes, thinly sliced crosswise
- 1 T. extra virgin olive oil
- ½ t. dried oregano
- 4 T. fresh basil, snipped, divided use
- salt and pepper to taste
- 12 thin slices mozzarella cheese (about the size of bread slice)

1. Preheat oven to 425.
2. Put tomato slices in dish and sprinkle with olive oil, oregano, 1 T. basil, salt and pepper.
3. Marinate about 30 minutes.
4. Butter one side of bread and put buttered side down on baking sheet.
5. Layer, on top of bread, the cheese, then the tomato slice.
6. Bake til brown on bottom and cheese is melted (about 5-10 minutes).
7. Garnish with 3 T. fresh basil.

Serves 6

PEPPERONI CHEESE PUFFS

from DENISE

My family is made up of a majority of males. They aren't crazy about "pretty food". So, this appetizer is perfect for them. It's especially great for football parties or late night movies.

My boys, spence and Price

- 1¼ cups water
- ⅓ cup shortening
- 1½ cups flour
- 4 eggs
- ¾ cup pepperoni (finely chopped)
- ¾ cup pecorino, romano or parmesan cheese, finely shredded
- 2 T. snipped parsley (fresh of course)
- ⅛ t. garlic powder
- ⅛ t. pepper
- garlic salt (to taste)

1. Preheat oven to 450.
2. Grease 2 baking sheets. (Use large sheets.)
3. In a large saucepan, combine the water and the shortening and bring it to a boil.
4. Next, add flour to the boiling water, stirring vigorously as you do so. You'll need to stir while you are cooking until the mixture starts to form a ball.
5. Remove your balled mixture and place in large bowl.
6. Let cool for 10 min.
7. At this point, add the eggs, one at a time.
8. Using a wooden spoon, beat each egg into the mixture very well.
9. Then, stir in the pepperoni and cheese, the parsley, garlic powder, and the pepper.
10. Just like you would with cookie dough, drop pepperoni dough using a rounded teaspoon about 2 inches apart onto prepared baking sheets.
11. All that's left to do is bake these for 15 to 17 min or until they are a beautiful golden brown.
12. Transfer to a wire rack and serve warm.

Serving suggestions:
Brush the top of the puffs with garlic butter-right before taking out of the oven.
Serve with a side of ranch or spaghetti sauce (OR BOTH!!!).

This appetizer recipe makes 48 delicious Pepperoni Cheese Puffs.
(You may want to double the recipe!)

PINE TOP TEA

from LEIGH

There is a family dispute as to whether this was Grandmother or Granddaddy Ivester's recipe so we'll just call it Pine Top Tea (this was their home address). There is no argument, however, on how delicious and sweet this traditional beverage tastes!

As Southern children, we were weaned off milk and went straight to drinking iced tea. There was always a pitcher of sweet tea in the refrigerator. We didn't keep liters of soda in the fridge. Coca-Colas (the ice cold small bottles, of course) were treats we got at Uncle Reese's store. Maybe the orange juice was added to the recipe so we could get a little vitamin C in the diet! You can rest assured that this refreshing drink will be the talk around the "tea cooler."

- 1 gallon water
- 4 large Lipton tea bags
- 2 cups sugar
- 2 heaping T. frozen orange juice concentrate
- 1 heaping T. frozen lemonade concentrate
- juice of half a lemon

Birthplace of Pine Top Tea

1. Brew tea according to instructions on box using one gallon of water.
2. Stir in all ingredients and add ice.

Serves 8-10

MINT JULEP

from DENISE

Last summer, my family spent two weeks in Oklahoma visiting all of our grandparents and cousins. One of our favorite stops was at my cousin Brent's house in Enid, OK. His family lives in a beautiful restored house with all kinds of character. Brent married his high school sweetheart, Marcy. She truly has the gift of hospitality. It was a hot summer day and she offered us this wonderfully refreshing drink. I have been making it ever since. It's great to have a pitcher made up to share with your neighbors or girlfriends as you sit on the porch for a chat.

- 3½ cups water
- 3½ cups sugar
- 6 oz. orange juice frozen concentrate
- 12 oz. lemonade frozen concentrate
- 1½ handfuls mint leaves (Which, of course, she had in her beautiful garden. I have to go buy them!)

1. Bring water and sugar to boil.
2. Add cans of concentrated orange juice and lemonade.
3. Let mixture reheat and pour over mint leaves.
4. Cover and let steep for at least 4 hours. (overnight is best)
5. Strain.
6. Use ¼ cup of mint concentrate to glass of crushed ice.
7. Finish filling glass with Ginger Ale, 7-Up, or any lemon-lime drink.

Serves 6-8

Marcy and Denise

I love appetizers because they always mean that I am having company! And you can actually eat as much as you want since the bites are so small...

— DENISE

GOAT CHEESE SPREAD

from DENISE

I know what you are thinking because I thought the same thing, "I'm not eating something that has the name GOAT in it." (Sorry to be a little gross, but POG commonly refers to goat cheese as "stinky feet cheese.") However, this cheese spread is wonderful. I don't host a lot of "fine dining" experiences at my house. My family tends to stick with the typical football-watching food, but this is a wonderful appetizer to serve at the beginning of a lovely, sophisticated evening. You can serve it with crackers in the family room or with French bread at the dinner table. Super yummy!

- 16 oz. cream cheese, softened
- 8 oz. goat cheese
- 2 garlic cloves, minced
- 4 t. chopped fresh oregano
  (or 1¼ t. dried oregano)
- ⅛ t. freshly ground pepper
- ¼ cup basil pesto
- ½ cup sun-dried tomatoes in oil,
  drained and chopped
- French bread slices or crackers

1. Process first five ingredients in a food processor until smooth.
2. Spread ⅓ of cheese mixture in a plastic wrap-lined 8x4 inch loaf pan.
3. Top with pesto.
4. Spread ⅓ cheese mixture over pesto.
5. Sprinkle with sun-dried tomatoes; top with remaining cheese mixture.
6. Cover and chill 8 hours.
7. Invert spread on a serving plate, discarding plastic wrap.
8. Garnish, if desired.
9. Serve with French bread slices or crackers.

Serves 12-16

a quick POINT

Although we have varying degrees of cooking expertise, one thing we all have in common is that we love to entertain. We have a lot of friends and family coming in and out of our homes and you just never know when a party will break out! These are some of our favorite store-bought appetizers that we keep on hand for such an occasion:

SHELLEY:
Mexican Layered Dip from Costco
I say why bother when you can buy it that cheap!

Hummus
I buy it in different flavors and serve it with pita chips and sliced red bell pepper.

LEIGH:
Edamame (aka soybeans-unshelled) from Kroger's Private Selection brand
I heat it up in the microwave and then place it in my really pretty ceramic strainer (for beautiful presentation). I just add kosher salt on top and serve it at parties. This is a REAL finger food and with everyone being so concerned with carb intake, it's always a winner!

DENISE:
Spinach Artichoke Dip from Publix
I just put it in a pretty dish, sprinkle some Paprika on it and bake for about 15 or 20 minutes. You can serve it with crackers, pita chips or tortilla chips. It looks and tastes like you made it yourself!

APPLE DIP

from SHELLEY

Now, I know full well that you can buy those little tubs of Caramel Dip in the fruit section of your grocery store, especially when Fall comes around and everyone is craving apple this and apple that! This is another one of my mom's recipes and once you make it, you will never buy one of those plastic tubs again!

- 8 oz. cream cheese, softened
- ¾ cup brown sugar, packed
- 1 T. vanilla
- ½ cup chopped peanuts

1. Mix together above four ingredients.
2. Serve with apple wedges. (Pretty at Christmas time to use red and green apples.)

Serves 8

HAM DELIGHTS

from LEIGH

My mom and my sister Dana often make these. (Yes, my sister's name is Dana and my husband's name is Dana. "Dana girl" and "Dana boy" is often how they are referred to. And would you believe Denise has a sister named Dayna too? Crazy huh?). These are great for tailgating. I prefer them warm but they are still "delightful" at room temperature. Give 'em a try!

- ½ cup butter, melted
- 2 T. dry mustard
- ½ t. Worcestershire sauce
- 1 t. poppy seeds
- 3 green onions, chopped or ¼ t. onion salt (optional)
- 1 pound honey ham, chopped
- 8 oz. grated Swiss cheese
- 2 packs of heat & serve dinner rolls (small rolls)

1. Preheat oven to 375.
2. Combine first 5 ingredients.
3. Stir in ham and cheeses.
4. Place 1 t. filling in center of each roll. Place back in pan.
5. Cover rolls with aluminum foil, and heat for 15 to 20 minutes.

(For a quicker preparation method: You can also slice entire pack of rolls with a large knife and remove top. Spread mixture over bottom layer of rolls. Return top layer, cover with foil and bake.)

Serves 10-12

Leigh with her sister and husband

BLEU CHEESE SPREAD

from SHELLEY

I fully trust my mother in all things, this recipe included. Now I must tell you, I DESPISE bleu cheese. I cannot even deal with the fact that some of you actually EAT this stuff, and furthermore, enjoy it. There is something about the smell and look. I don't know. It's weird. There, I said it! Now that I've had my bleu cheese rant, I must admit my mother swears by this recipe. She says it's great for a party and everyone always gives it rave reviews, at least those who are in the "I Love Bleu Cheese for Some Reason" Club. Enjoy! (If you must!)

- 12 oz. crumbled bleu cheese
- 3 large cloves garlic, crushed
- ½ cup olive oil
- 4 T. red wine vinegar
- 2 T. lemon juice
- 1 cup red onion, finely chopped
- 1 cup minced fresh cilantro

1. Put bleu cheese in bottom of serving dish.
2. Mix garlic and olive oil together
   and drizzle over cheese.
3. Combine vinegar, lemon juice, onion
   and cilantro and spread over the cheese.
4. Cover and chill in refrigerator at least 2 hrs.
5. Serve with various crackers.
   (Or you could use Granny Smith apple slices.)

Serves 8-10

SHELLEY'S SUCCOTASH DIP

from SHELLEY

Succotash is a savory concoction of peas and corn. This particular recipe calls for field peas and I know you may be asking, "What are field peas?" They are in the canned vegetable section and they are like small black-eyed peas with tiny pieces of green beans in them. All I can find are the seasoned ones, which work fine. People ask me if I lace this with something addictive because they can't stop eating it!

- Two 15.8 oz. cans field peas with snaps, rinsed and drained
- Two 11 oz. cans white shoe peg corn, drained
- Two 10 oz. cans diced tomatoes with green chiles
- 14½ oz. can diced tomatoes
- 6 green onions, sliced
- 16 oz. bottle zesty Italian dressing
- 3 garlic cloves, minced
- 1 T. finely chopped parsley

1. Stir together all ingredients.
2. Cover and chill for 8 hours.
3. Drain before serving.
4. Serve with corn chips.

Serves 12-14

menu SUGGESTIONS

For a casual gathering, such as a football-watching party we suggest: Meetballs, Kickin' Bacon & Chicken Bites, Pepperoni Puffs, Shelley's Mom's Salsa (from Mexican Night) and a big plate of Julie's New & Improved Chocolate Chip Cookies (from Dessert).

For a nicer occasion, such as a wedding shower we suggest: Onion Souffle' with good crackers, Bruschetta appetizer, Ham Delights cut into bite size pieces, Toasted Pecans served in a pretty bowl, Glazed Tea Cake (from Dessert) and Mint Julep.

KICKIN' BACON & CHICKEN BITES

from LEIGH

YEE HAW!!!!!! Can you hear me now? I said - YEEEEE HAW!!!! I had my first bite of a "kickin' bacon & chicken bite" just this year and I will never go back to just ordinary nuggets. These are quite the hubby pleasers, as in, "Honey, PLEASE make more!" Our friend Julie surprised us with these one night at the bus (on the "Come Alive" tour) and the band and crew DEVOURED them, even knowing they had jalapeños in them. Julie brought them to us right out of the oven but as the drive continued, they were still delicious cold. This recipe would be absolutely perfect for any party with lots and lots of testosterone. I don't even need to say that we love them, too. POG and anything wrapped in bacon is a "no-brainer." (Julie wants me to tell you that she got this recipe from her friend Angie. Turns out that Angie and I go to the same church! Small world, huh?)

- 1½ pounds raw chicken breast – cut into bite-size pieces
- 1 pound bacon
- 1 bottle pickled, sliced jalapeños
- Fajita seasoning (can be found in spice aisle)

1. Preheat oven to 375.
2. Put one slice of jalapeño on a piece of chicken.
3. Take ⅓ piece of bacon and wrap around chicken and jalapeño.
4. Secure with a toothpick and place in 9x13 baking dish.
5. Repeat assembly until baking dish is full.
6. Generously sprinkle fajita seasoning over chicken & bacon bites.
7. Bake for 1 hour – or until bacon is well done. (You can pour some of the grease off half way through.)
8. Remove bites from dish and place on paper towels to remove some of the grease.

Serves 8-10

CHURCH LADY'S CHEESE BALL

from SHELLEY

This cheese ball was in our dressing room at a church on one of the many stops during our Christmas Tour last year. I wish I could remember exactly where we were and who made it for us, but hey, at least I got the recipe! The three of us girls had eaten the whole dang ball by ourselves by the end of the show!

- 16 oz. cream cheese, softened
- 2 cups grated cheddar cheese
- 1 T. Worcestershire sauce
- 1 T. diced onion
- 1 t. garlic powder
- parsley flakes or granulated nuts (optional)

1. Mix ingredients together at low speed with mixer.
2. Shape cheese ball and roll in parsley flakes or granulated nuts if desired

Serves 12-14 (or 3 POG members!)

The Christmas Tour

shelley and Caroline backstage

singing while stuffed with cheese ball

SPINACH & BACON DIP

from DENISE

Dips are my favorite thing to eat. I'm not a huge fan of vegetables, but if you add them to a dip or serve them with a dip, I'm all about them. We had the opportunity to do a cooking segment on hearitfirst.com and they wanted us to do some type of spinach or artichoke dip. I wanted to try to find something a little different than what I've eaten at so many parties. I wish I could tell you where I found this recipe, but I honestly cannot remember. However, it would be a shame if I didn't pass it on to you because it's soooooo delicious. Spinach has NEVER tasted so good!

- 1 lb. bacon, cooked and crumbled
- 10 oz. package frozen spinach, thawed and squeezed dry
- 1 medium onion, chopped
- 2 T. butter
- 24 oz. cream cheese, softened
- 5 oz. shredded parmesan cheese (in the nice section of cheeses, ya know, the real stuff!)
- 1 cup shredded mozzarella cheese
- ½ cup of mayonnaise

1. Preheat oven to 350.
2. Sauté onions in butter 'til soft.
3. Combine onions with all other ingredients in large bowl.
4. Mix together with mixer.
5. Bake 30 minutes 'til bubbly.
6. Serve with crackers, pita chips or tortilla chips.

Serves 14-16

CHAPTER TWO

SO, NOT ALL SALADS ARE BLAH

If the first thing that comes to mind when you think "salad" is dieting, then you are not alone! We can give you our guarantee right now that you will not find these salads on any weight loss program anywhere! They are all beautifully decadent. Go ahead, splurge on a little salad!

KARRI'S GREAT GRAPE SALAD

from DENISE

For years, my family has spent many special occasions out at my friend Karri's farm. She has always invited us to spend holidays at her house when we couldn't go to our own because of my POG schedule. Karri loves TV cooking channels as much as Shelley does and will experiment with things to try for our get-togethers. She made this particular grape salad for my birthday lunch that she hosted at her house.

- 4 oz. sour cream
- 4 oz. cream cheese, softened
- 2 cups grapes, halved (you can do red and green - I prefer just green)
- 1 t. vanilla
- ½ cup brown sugar
- ½ cup chopped pecans

1. Mix sour cream, cream cheese and vanilla.
2. Blend in grapes and put in 8x8 dish.
3. Mix brown sugar and pecans and cover the entire grape mixture.
4. Chill for at least an hour.

Serves 6
(You can double this recipe
if you want to make a 9x13 pan)

SUN-DRIED TOMATO PASTA SALAD

from SHELLEY

This salad is such a great addition to any cookout or get-together. Especially when it's summertime and the tomatoes are ripe! It's also pretty to look at. It has lots of red and green with basil and two kinds of tomatoes! Sometimes, if I'm hosting a lunchtime or afternoon baby shower, I will do chicken salad on croissants with this pasta salad for a light meal.

- 16 oz. box penne pasta
- 8 oz. bottle of zesty Italian dressing
- 2 large tomatoes, chopped
- 7 oz. jar of sun-dried tomatoes in oil, drained and chopped
- 8 oz. crumbled feta cheese
- ½ cup fresh basil, chopped

1. Cook pasta according to package directions.
2. Rinse in cold water.
3. Add remaining ingredients and chill for at least 2 hours.

Serves 8-10

YUMMY SALAD

from LEIGH

This is not an original recipe but the name is original. Denise calls it the "yummy salad" and I would completely agree. Shelley has a bottomless pit of recipes and when my parents were coming into town I needed something special. Shelley was the one to call. "Help," I cried. This is the salad she said would be great with any entree. Can I just say, my family absolutely raved about it, so much so that it WAS and still IS their request when they come to town. Sadly, after reading this cookbook they will know the truth: I am not the cooking genius they thought I was! That's okay. The satisfaction is in knowing everyone enjoys each bite!

Dressing:
- ½ cup sugar
- ¼ cup white vinegar
- 2 T. apple cider vinegar
- 2 cloves garlic, minced
- ½ cup oil

Salad:
- 6 cups sweet butter lettuce
- 1 can (8.25 oz) mandarin orange (drained)
- ½ cup slivered almonds (heated at 350 degrees for 2 to 5 min)
- Purple onion (chopped)
- Avocado (optional)

1. In small bowl with a tightly fitting lid, combine sugar, vinegars, and garlic.
2. Add oil and fit lid on bowl. Shake vigorously to combine.
3. In large bowl, combine salad greens, oranges, almonds, onion, and avocado.
4. Drizzle with salad dressing just before serving.
5. Toss gently.

Serves 6-8

COOKING CLASS #2

CONCOCTING YOUR OWN DRESSING: It's sort of like a science experiment – it starts with a base and an acid!

1. Measure ⅓ to ½ cup of a base into jar or bowl

   Base:
   Olive oil | Vegetable oil | Canola oil |
   Mayonnaise (add 1 or 2 T. to oil for creamy dressing)

2. Add ⅓ to ½ cup of an acid

   Acid:
   Balsamic vinegar | White vinegar
   Apple cider vinegar
   Red wine vinegar | Lemon juice

3. Have fun adding as many extra ingredients as you want!

   Add-ins:
   1 ½ t. Minced onion | 1 T. Poppy seeds | 1 T. Sesame seeds |
   ¼ t. Paprika | ½ t. Garlic powder | 2 t. Soy sauce |
   ½ t. Worcestershire sauce |
   1 T. Sugar or 1-2 packs artificial sweetener
   (REALLY makes dressing tasty)

4. Place lid on jar or bowl and shake vigorously.

Examples of finished dressings:
⅓ cup olive oil, 2 T. mayo, ⅓ cup Balsamic vinegar, 2 t. soy sauce, 1 T. sugar

Another good one is ½ cup oil, ⅓ cup sugar, ½ cup apple cider vinegar, 1 T. poppy seeds, 2 T. sesame seeds, 1 ½ t. minced onion, ½ t. Worcestershire sauce, ¼ t. paprika

NANNY'S CRANBERRY SALAD

from DENISE

My grandmother, Miriam, whom I called Nanny, was one of those amazing women who always had something she could throw together. My grandpa was a pastor and you just never knew who would come home with him for Sunday dinner or even to live with them for a while. If she didn't feed you while you were there, she felt like she had not been a good hostess. I hope that somewhere down the line I will develop some of her characteristics. I often think about the times that I visited with her. They were always so calm and relaxing. She offered advice when asked, but would just let me talk about whatever. She made me feel God's peace in her presence. I want to be like that.

On holidays, there was always way more food than we needed because that's just the way she did it. Not a Thanksgiving went by without a Cranberry Congealed Salad. My sister Dayna has tweaked this recipe, but I always think of Nanny when I eat it.

- 1 cup fresh cranberries, ground
- ¾ cup boiling water
- 1 fresh orange, peeled
- 8 oz. can crushed pineapple, drained
- 3 oz. package raspberry gelatin
- ½ cup pecans, chopped
- ½ cup sugar

1. In food processor, grind cranberries and orange; set aside.
2. Mix gelatin, boiling water and sugar. Stir until sugar dissolves.
3. Cool slightly then add cranberries, orange, pineapple and pecans.
4. Pour into 9x13 casserole dish.
5. Chill until firm (at least 4 hours).

Serves 10-12

Papa and Nanny

SUPER WILTED SALAD

from SHELLEY

I grew up going to a small Lutheran church in Little Rock, Arkansas. I remember on many Sundays we would go to a little restaurant after church for lunch called "The Faded Rose." A lot of the adults would always get something called "Super Wilted Salad" and I thought that sounded so disgusting. I mean, who wants their salad wilted, seriously?? Eventually, they printed the recipe in the local newspaper, The Arkansas Democrat, and my mom started making the salad at home. I ended up loving it and it's a nice change from a normal old salad with Italian dressing when you are having spaghetti or lasagna.

Salad:
- 1 head iceberg lettuce, chopped
- 1 head romaine lettuce, chopped
- 15 oz. can artichoke hearts, quartered
- 15 oz. can hearts of palm, sliced
- ½ cup grated Parmesan cheese
- 2 oz. jar of pimento, drained
- 1 purple onion, sliced thin

Dressing:
- One packet of dry zesty Italian dressing
- red wine vinegar
- light olive oil

1. Follow directions on dressing packet using red wine vinegar and olive oil in amounts shown.
2. Mix all ingredients and chill.
3. Add dressing and toss thirty minutes before serving.

Serves 10-12

a quick POINT

POG is not a fan of green bell peppers! (When they make an appearance in our recipes, we consider them optional.)

LEIGH'S CHICKEN SALAD

from LEIGH

Picnic time! No rhyme, no reason and barely a recipe, but it sure is yummy!

- 10.5 oz. canned chicken, drained
- ½ cup cream cheese, softened
- ½ cup mayonnaise (Have I mentioned Duke's is my favorite?!)
- ½ cup grapes, cut in half
- 1 Granny Smith apple, cut in small bites with skin left on
- ½ wedge of freshly squeezed lemon juice
- ½ cup of sliced almonds, toasted
- salt and pepper to taste

1. Mix ingredients together.
2. Chill overnight.
   (or at least 4 hours)

It's also delicious with your favorite crackers!!

Serves 4

HIDDEN VALLEY
HOT POTATO SALAD

from DENISE

I love potatoes and I love ranch dressing. So combine the two together and you get a wonderful potato salad. My sister Dayna happens to be a really good cook. Her husband is a music minister. In fact, my sisters married brothers and they are both music ministers. How cool is that? Therefore, they have been to MANY church functions. There is never a church function without food, so they taste lots of recipes. This potato salad is one that Dayna has taken to a lot of pot luck dinners.

- 2 lbs. small red potatoes, cubed
- ½ cup green onions, sliced
- 1 pkg. Hidden Valley Ranch Original Salad Dressing, prepared as directed on pkg.
- Paprika or black pepper, optional

1. Prepare salad dressing and add onions, then refrigerate about 30 minutes.
2. Boil potatoes until tender and drain.
3. While still warm, gently toss with salad dressing.
4. Dust with paprika or pepper.

Serve warm or at room temperature.

Serves 6-8

CRUNCHY ROMAINE TOSS

from SHELLEY

This salad is totally my signature standby. There are lots of versions floating around out there, but this one has never failed me. There is just something about putting a yummy, sweet dressing on romaine that makes salad seem more like a dessert, which is never a bad thing.

A few years back, Michael Passons started traveling with us. He is one of the founding members of the group Avalon. He is a wonderful singer, piano player and friend. The addition of his voice and incredible piano talents really added an enjoyable element to our live shows. Being a bachelor, Michael is always up for a home cooked meal. So, whenever we have him over, he always requests this salad. It's his favorite. I have made this salad on many occasions when my neighbors come over to eat, too. We will be totally full after dinner, but Kirsten and I will stand at the counter and stick our forks right into the serving bowl to finish this salad off. It's just simply too good to waste! Try it, you'll see!

Sweet and Sour Dressing:
- 1 cup vegetable oil
- 1 cup sugar
- ½ cup white wine vinegar
- 3 t. soy sauce

1. Whisk ingredients together.

Salad:
- 1 cup walnuts, chopped
- 1 pkg. Ramen noodles, uncooked, broken up
- 4 T. unsalted butter
- 1 bunch fresh broccoli, coarsely chopped
- 1 head romaine lettuce, washed and broken up
- 4 green onions, chopped
- 1 cup sweet and sour dressing (recipe above)

Michael Passons and Shelley and the crunchy romaine masterpiece

2. Brown walnuts and noodles in butter.
3. Cool and drain on paper towel.
4. Combine remaining ingredients and toss.

Serves 6-8

I love salads because of the crunch.
If it ain't got a crunch, I don't wanna eat it.
— LEIGH

TURKEY & BACON SALAD

from LEIGH

This is a great option for lunch or a light dinner. I think I like this so much because of the crunch in each bite!

- 5 slices of bacon (I use low sodium bacon)
- 2 cups sugar snap peas
- ½ cup mayonnaise (Do I need to remind you to use Duke's mayo? It's the best!!)
- 1 T. dijon-style mustard
- 1 T. cider vinegar
- 1 T. snipped fresh dill (love me some dill)
- 1 small head of romaine coarsely chopped or torn
- 8 oz. roast turkey breast, cut into strips (or use your favorite deli turkey if short on time)

1. Cook bacon the way you desire. (Microwave is always my choice.)
2. Cook peas, covered, in boiling, salted water 2 minutes or until crisp-tender; then drain.
3. Crumble one slice of bacon, set aside. Break remaining into pieces.
4. In a bowl combine mayo, mustard, vinegar and dill.
5. Stir in crumbled bacon.
6. Arrange romaine on each plate. Add peas, turkey strips and bacon pieces.
7. Drizzle with dressing.

Serves 6-8

a quick POINT

Get A Little Nutty: here's a tip on how to make any salad seem gourmet!

Sugared Almonds
a. Put ¾ cup of almonds (whole, sliced or slivered) in skillet.
b. Pour ⅓ cup of sugar over almonds.
c. Heat on medium high, stirring occasionally (about 5 minutes).
d. When sugar starts to liquify, stir constantly until all nuts are covered in glaze (about 1 minute).
e. Do not overcook – nuts burn easily.
f. Pour nuts into aluminum pan and let them harden.
g. Nuts will be crisp and can be crumbled over salad.

CURRY CHICKEN SALAD

from DENISE

I never knew that I liked the flavor of curry until I tasted this Curry Chicken Salad. It was served at my first baby shower for my son, Spence, back in Norman, Oklahoma. We had a sweet time at my mom's house with all of the church ladies I grew up knowing and loving. They taught me in the nursery, Sunday school, church choir, etc. Now I was having my own baby and felt a little sad that I wouldn't be raising my children under their care. However, they gave me great advice about being a mom and have shown me through their lives what being a Godly mother and woman looks like.

When I host baby showers for my friends here in Nashville, this is one of the things I always offer to make. You can even be cute and creative and serve it on potato bread, which has a yellow tint to it. Cut the bread in the shape of a little chick by using a cookie cutter. It's also really pretty in a bowl lined with lettuce.

- 8 boneless chicken breasts, cooked and cubed
- 1½ cups white grapes, halved
- 4 oz. package sliced almonds
- 1 cup chopped green apples
- 1 cup diced celery
- 2 cups of mayonnaise
- 1 T. curry powder
- 1 t. lemon juice

1. In large bowl, combine chicken, grapes, apples, celery, and almonds.
2. Mix well.
3. In separate bowl, blend mayo, curry, and lemon juice thoroughly.
4. Pour over chicken mixture and toss lightly.
5. If it doesn't seem like there is enough mayo just add a little more.
6. Chill well.

Serves 16

ASIAN CABBAGE SLAW

from SHELLEY

There are not a lot of people who genuinely make me laugh, but I am very thankful for the few in my life who do. I got this recipe from one of those people. Jill and I have been friends for years, and lots of people would say we are rotten when we are together. The truth is, we just aren't afraid to say what everyone else is thinking! She is a frequent dinner guest at my house and is affectionately known by my daughter as "Jilly Jill." Some friendships come and go, but she is one of those girls that I get my "fix" of most every day. It's sorta like eatin' and breathin'. I love those kinds of friends and I'm thankful she's in my life. It's good to know there is someone else out there just like me!

Now, about this salad: the other thing Jill and I have in common is our love for all things "food." We have shared many recipes over the years and this is one of my most requested favorites. Even though it's "Asian," it goes great with any meal. And even my husband, who would NEVER put a bite of cabbage in his mouth, loves this salad. It's crispy and resembles a slaw, only more flavorful and hearty!

Salad:
- 1 head Napa cabbage, sliced thin
- 1 bunch green onions, chopped fine

Chill in large plastic zipper bag together for an hour

- 1 pkg. ramen noodles, crushed
- 2 T. sesame seeds
- ½ cup slivered almonds
- ½ stick margarine

1. Sauté ramen noodles, sesame seeds and almonds in margarine until light brown.
2. Drain on paper towel.

Dressing:
- ½ cup oil
- ¼ cup white vinegar
- 1 T. soy sauce
- ⅓ cup sugar

- *shelley and Jilly Jill*

3. Whisk dressing together and refrigerate.
4. Mix together vegetables and ramen noodle mixture before serving.
5. Toss with dressing to coat.

Serves 6-8

AMY GRANT'S RED & GREEN ROMAINE SALAD

from LEIGH

When we started talking about salads for our cookbook, our friend Julie told us about a really good one that she has been making for years. She calls it "Amy Grant Salad" because she learned it from Amy. Apparently Amy is as talented in the kitchen as she is in the studio! We were so honored when she agreed to let us put her salad (and her pot roast!) in our cookbook. I said, "Well, why don't I tell the story of the first time I met Amy?"

We were out on her Christmas tour and we were in Portland, Oregon. She came into our POG dressing room to say "Hello." She was so beautiful and extremely kind. (Of course she was.) I will never forget the enormous compliment she gave me when she said, "Leigh, you are really present in my ears. You have great intonation!" I was humbled because that was a sweet way of saying, "You sing in tune!" Hee hee. How 'bout that? I wonder if she would compliment me on my cooking too?

Amy and Leigh

- ½ head red romaine lettuce, chopped
- ½ head green romaine lettuce, chopped
- 2 or 3 roma tomatoes, chopped
- ½ bunch green onions, sliced (optional – Vince doesn't like onions!)
- 1 packet dry Italian dressing (Amy likes the one that comes with a cruet, which is a bottle used to make dressing)
- Balsamic vinegar
- Vegetable Oil (Amy used to use olive oil, but she thinks vegetable oil has a lighter taste)

1. Follow directions on dressing packet using Balsamic vinegar and vegetable oil.
2. Combine lettuce, tomatoes and onions in large bowl
3. Add dressing and toss.

Serves 6-8

CUCUMBER SALAD

from LEIGH

This cucumber salad smells SO good. The crazy thing is, I don't eat cucumbers! Whether I eat it or not I still have to make it because my husband and everybody else LOVES it! It is a staple during the hot summer months and a great salad option.

- 2 large cucumbers, peeled, seeded and chopped
- 1 tomato peeled and chopped
- 1 small bell pepper chopped
- 1 small onion chopped
- salt and pepper to taste
- zesty Italian dressing

1. Mix cucumbers, tomatoes, bell pepper and onion together and season as desired with salt and pepper.
2. Coat well with zesty Italian salad dressing. (I use Ken's.)
3. Marinate 2-3 hours or overnight. The longer it marinates the better.

Serves 4-6

STRAWBERRY PRETZEL SALAD

from DENISE

I had never heard of this until I moved to Tennessee and started having Thanksgiving out at the home of our good friends, the Stills. Ms. Ann always makes her Strawberry Pretzel Salad. I still can't decide which category to put this in. Is it a side dish, a salad or a dessert? Whatever it is, all I know is that it is good! It's a little sweet and a little salty. Nothing is better than that!

Crust:
- 2 cups pretzels crushed
- ½ cup sugar
- ¾ cup margarine melted

1. Preheat oven to 350.
2. Mix above ingredients and spread into a well-greased 9 x 13 inch pan.
3. Bake for 10 minutes.
4. Let cool.

Filling:
- 8 oz. cream cheese, softened
- 1 cup sugar
- 10 oz. Cool Whip

1. Mix together and spread on top of pretzel crust.
2. Chill for 1-2 hours before adding topping.

Topping:
- 6 oz. package strawberry gelatin
- 20 oz. frozen strawberries with juice
- 2 cups boiling water

1. Dissolve gelatin in boiling water.
2. Add strawberries.
3. Let partially set. (You may even want to put in fridge for just a little while.)
4. When gelatin is partially firm, spread on top of cream cheese layer and chill thoroughly (3-4 hours).

Denise and Ms. Ann and Strawberry Pretzel Salad

Serves 15

ROMAINE AND FRUIT SALAD WITH CITRUS/POPPY SEED VINAIGRETTE

from DENISE

This is what I make almost every time I am in charge of making a salad for our community group or a party. It's always a hit at outdoor barbeques because it's refreshing and cool. It is easy, pretty and yummy, as well.

Vinaigrette:
¼ cup orange juice
2 T. white wine vinegar
2 green onions, chopped
⅓ cup sugar
¼ t. salt
⅓ cup oil
1 T. poppy seeds

Salad:
8 cups torn romaine lettuce (about ⅔ head)
1 cup cubed honeydew melon
1 cup cubed cantaloupe
1 cup halved strawberries

1. In blender or food processor, combine orange juice, vinegar, onions, sugar and salt.
2. Cover; blend well.
3. With machine running, slowly add oil, blending until thick and smooth.
4. Add poppy seeds; blend a few seconds to mix.
5. In large serving bowl, combine all salad ingredients; toss to mix. Pour dressing over salad; toss to coat

Serves 10

DIANNE'S POTATO SALAD

from LEIGH

John Mays is the wonderful man who discovered Point of Grace almost 20 years ago, and signed us to our first record deal. To know John, is to love him! He is very tall and when I first met him many years ago I was expecting him to have this large voice to go along with his height. However, when he spoke his voice was so peaceful. John is such an important part of the Point Of Grace family tree. You might even say he is the sturdy trunk. Well, you know the old sayin', "behind every great man is a better woman!" Ha Ha! When John was our A&R man (the guy who helps us find our great songs) during the recording process for our "I Choose You" record, he and his wife, Dianne, graciously invited us over to dine with them. We quickly learned that Dianne has the gift of hospitality. The meal and fellowship was, of course, fabulous and the more time we spent with Dianne the more we realized what a great cook she is. Dianne Mays, "I Choose You" for a potato salad recipe! (We left this recipe in her words!)

Salad:
- 6 Potatoes (I use the large baking potatoes from Costco and usually bake 1 large potato for every 2 people.)
- 1 onion, chopped
- 1 cup sweet relish
- 4 hard-boiled eggs
- salt and pepper to taste
- paprika

1. Wash the potatoes and wrap in foil.
2. Bake at 350 until they are soft.
3. Take them out and let them cool enough so that they don't burn your hands.
4. Peel potatoes and cut into pretty good size hunks.
5. Add chopped onion and relish.
6. Salt and pepper to taste.

Dressing:
- 2 cups mayonnaise
- 2 T. red wine vinegar
- 1 T. sugar
- ¼ to ½ cup milk

1. Mix together mayonnaise, red wine vinegar and sugar.
2. Thin with milk.
3. Add to potato mixture and stir.
4. Slice boiled egg on top. (This makes it easier for John to pick it out!)
5. Sprinkle with paprika.

Serves 12

CHAPTER THREE

SO, SOUP'S ON!

Soup is almost as much fun to make as it is to eat! With all the slicing and dicing and sautéing involved, you really feel like a chef. It is easy to experiment and alter the measurements to make it your own. Plus, there is nothing like a big pot of soup simmering on the stove to welcome your family home on a cold winter night. It definitely gives casserole a run for its money as the world's greatest comfort food! That's why we like to eat it year 'round.

THE HOWARDS' GOLDEN POTATO SOUP

from SHELLEY

I cook for my little family a fair amount, but it is always a treat for someone to cook for me! My neighbor Rob shares my love for all things food, so he is the first to appreciate and praise most things I bring them to eat. On occasion, Rob makes a few specialties of his own and we are usually the lucky recipients of his efforts. When I asked him to submit a couple of recipes for this cookbook, he emailed me a list of his favorites and I quickly chose this potato soup as one of my choices to share with you. It was a bit of a chore for him to actually figure out the exact ingredient amounts for this one since he is like me in that he cooks by taste as he goes! Apparently, Rob's sister Susan must have rubbed off on him because she is quite the cook herself. In fact, at one point he actually did credit this recipe to her, so we're just calling it "The Howards' soup!" It's rich and creamy and very UN-DIETARY!! But hey, who cares about that? I'm sure as heck not gonna start counting calories now. I'm a cookbook author!

- 9 Yukon Gold potatoes, diced
- 7 chicken bouillon cubes
- ½ cup butter
- 3 stalks celery, thinly sliced
- 1 medium Spanish (yellow) onion, diced
- 3 cups half & half
- 3 cups milk
- ½ cup heavy whipping cream
- ½ pouch instant butter & herb mashed potato mix
- 4 T. flour
- 2 cups diced honey-glazed ham
- crumbled bacon
- scallions
- shredded cheese

Rob and Shelley

1. Place potatoes and bouillon cubes in a large pot (8 quart) and put in just enough water to cover the potatoes.
2. Bring to a boil until potatoes are tender.
3. While potatoes are cooking, sauté onions and celery in butter, do not brown.
4. When tender, add flour to make a roux. (a thick buttery base-see Cooking Class on page 60)
5. Add milk, half & half, heavy whipping cream, mashed potato mix and ham to the potatoes.
6. Bring to a boil, then add roux.
7. Simmer for 10-15 minutes.
8. Salt and pepper to taste.

Serve topped with crumbled bacon, scallions and shredded cheese.

Serves 8-10

BEEF STEW

from DENISE

One of my favorite things to eat on the road is Cracker Barrel's beef stew. I LOVE IT! (Especially in the fall and winter when it's dark and cold outside.) I looked and looked for a recipe that is comparable to it, so that I could make it at home. I finally found this one and it comes pretty close to my favorite stew. It is really good and it freezes well.

- 1 lb. stew meat
- 8 oz. can tomato sauce
- 1 bay leaf
- ¼ cup parsley flakes
- 1 t. basil
- 1 t. marjoram
- 4 to 6 cups water
- 8 potatoes, peeled and diced
- 8 carrots, peeled and diced
- 1 chopped onion
- 16 oz. can whole tomatoes
- 3 T. Worcestershire sauce
- 3 T. chili powder
- ¼ cup cooking sherry

1. Cook meat, tomato sauce, bay leaf, parsley, basil, marjoram, and water in large pot until meat is tender - about 1½ hours.
2. Add remaining ingredients except for sherry and cook until veggies are tender.
3. Add sherry 5 minutes before serving.

Serves 8-10

VEGETABLE SOUP

from LEIGH

You have to admit, not many of us get our daily allowance of vegetables. This soup recipe can help solve that very easily. Growing up, Mom made this soup more often in the cooler months. I had no idea as a kid that I was even eating vegetables. (I thought I was just eating soup.) Mom would clean out everything in her freezer, especially leftovers from Sunday dinners, put it in a pot with cabbage and stewed tomatoes and PRESTO - the best veggie soup in the world! Mom would fix cornbread to accompany the soup and after we were all full we would take another piece of cornbread and crumble it up in a glass of REALLY cold milk for dessert. It was so good! It makes me want it right now. Soup and cornbread is a heavenly combination for me.

- 28 oz. can crushed tomatoes
- 15 oz. can petite diced tomatoes w/ celery, onion and green pepper
- 2 cups cut corn
- 2 cups sliced okra (fresh or frozen)
- 2 cups butterbeans or peas
- 1 cup cabbage chopped fine
- 1 small onion chopped
- 1 potato diced
- 1 t. thyme
- 1 t. basil
- salt to taste
- pepper
- 2 T. vegetable oil
- dash tabasco sauce
- pinch sugar
- water

GREAT ADVICE FROM MY MOM!

LEIGH: The presentation is as important as the taste!" This is what Mom would say to Daddy when he tried to serve the food in the pan it was cooked in! That statement has stuck with me through the years and I always try to be mindful of presentation whenever possible.

1. Pour tomatoes with one 15 oz. can of water in dutch oven and simmer while preparing other ingredients.
2. Add each ingredient as prepared.
3. Stir ingredients together then add water to fill pot.
4. Bring soup mixture to a boil then turn on low and simmer 45 minutes.

Serves 10-12

SMOKED SAUSAGE SOUP

from DENISE

When my son Spence started kindergarten he met a little boy named George and they have been the best of friends ever since. The great thing about that was that I got to know George's mom, Beth. And we became instant friends. She was born and raised in Nashville and has all of her family right here in town. Her mom and dad (Momma and Pap) and her sister Denise have become like family. Pap has taken my boys fishing, Denise has loaned us tons of clothes that her boys have outgrown and Momma has shared her recipes and cheered Spence on from the stands at ballgames. I had this particular soup for the first time at the annual Halloween party. I think I ate 3 bowls that night. It has a nice little kick to warm you from the inside out.

- 4½ cups water
- 1 can (28 oz.) diced tomatoes
- 1 envelope onion soup mix
- 1 pkg. (9 oz.) frozen green beans
- 3 small carrots, peeled, halved and sliced
- 2 celery ribs, thinly sliced
- ½ t. dried oregano
- 1/8 t. hot sauce
- 1 lb. smoked sausage, halved, sliced and cooked
- 2½ cups frozen, shredded hash brown potatoes

1. Mix all ingredients except for sausage and hash browns.
2. Bring to a boil in pot. Then simmer 30 minutes.
3. After 30 minutes add the cooked smoked sausage and shredded hash brown potatoes.
4. Heat and simmer for 15 more minutes.

Serves 6-8

Denise, Spence, George and Beth

JEN'S CURRY CHICKEN LENTIL WITH SWEET POTATOES

from LEIGH

This recipe was developed by our friend Jennifer Cooke, who is Amy Grant's manager. She got the idea for it when she had lunch at this funky little coffee shop near Music Row one day. The soup of the day was vegan sweet potato curry lentil. Jen said it was so delicious that she became obsessed with the thought of trying to recreate it. Well, it's not vegan anymore since she added chicken, but it is still delicious!

- 2 medium sweet potatoes, peeled and cubed in ½ inch pieces
- 2 T. butter
- large sweet yellow onion, chopped
- ½ t. minced garlic
- 1½ T. curry powder
- 1 T. ginger
- 1 t. cumin
- 1 t. salt
- ⅛ t. red cayenne pepper
- dash of black pepper
- 3½ cups vegetable broth
- 6 cups water
- 16 oz. dry lentils
- 2 cups cooked chicken (diced)
- ½ cup of golden raisins

Amy and Jennifer

1. Melt 2 T. butter in large pot. Add sweet potatoes and onions.
2. Saute' til onions are soft (about 10 minutes).
3. Add ingredients from garlic through black pepper and cook for about 1 minute.
4. Add ingredients from vegetable broth through golden raisins, stirring until well mixed.
5. Bring to a slow boil and simmer for 40-50 minutes.

Serve over a generous portion of basmati rice.

Serves 8-10

TORTELLINI SOUP

from SHELLEY

This is a great soup for a cold winter night, especially when you don't have a lot of time to make a "homemade" meal that takes forever. It's also a great way to get some vegetables in your diet, but in a yummy way! Serve with a little buttery toasted bread and you've got yourself a tasty supper. The best part is that it's even better the next day!

- 3 T. olive oil
- 1 clove garlic, minced
- 3 stalks celery, chopped
- 3 carrots, peeled and chopped
- 1 onion, diced
- 10 oz. box frozen spinach (unthawed)
- 2 cans cream of chicken soup
- 2 cans water
- 32 oz. chicken broth
- Family size package of cheese or chicken tortellini, half-cooked

1. Put olive oil in the bottom of a large soup/stock pan.
2. Saute' garlic, celery, carrots and onions until tender.
3. Add frozen spinach. Break up block of spinach as you cook.
4. Continue to saute' until spinach thaws, then heats up.
5. Add cream of chicken soup and water.
6. Add chicken broth and then add tortellini.
7. Heat and serve.

* It's better to eat it a few hours after it's made so the broth soaks into the noodles! Better yet, make it the night before.

Serves 6-8

GREAT ADVICE FROM
MY MOM!

SHELLEY: Mom always says to prepare as much of the meal ahead of time as possible. I usually try to do that, and just the other day my good friend Michael gave me a great compliment. He said, "I don't understand where all your dirty dishes are when I come over for dinner. When I get here, the kitchen looks clean and the meal just appears...how do you do that??" I do try to clean as I go. I figure no one wants to see gross dishes with dried food remnants in them right before they eat!

BUTTERNUT SQUASH SOUP

from DENISE

A few years ago, we had the opportunity to travel and sing at the National "Women of Faith" Conferences. It was such a blessing to get to know the speakers and sit and listen to them give Godly wisdom. On occasion, we even had the chance to visit them in their homes. On one blessed day, we had the privilege to go hang out at Patsy Clairmont's house. She is QUITE the hostess. She even had toys out for our kids to play with. Her home is so charming and it was a wonderful day. Most wonderful days include some type of meal and she did not let us down. One of my favorite dishes was the Butternut Squash soup. After we left I had to email her and beg for the recipe. It's the kind of soup I love to eat curled up on the couch on a cold gloomy day.

- 6 bacon slices
- 1 large onion, chopped
- 2 celery ribs, chopped
- 1 Granny Smith apple, peeled and finely chopped
- 2 garlic cloves, chopped
- 4 (12 oz.) packages frozen butternut squash, thawed (or use 3 lbs. fresh, peeled, seeded and chopped)
- 32 oz. chicken broth
- 2 to 3 T. fresh lime juice
- 1½ T. honey
- 2 t. salt
- 1 t. black pepper
- ⅛ t. allspice
- ⅛ t. nutmeg
- ⅛ red pepper
- ¼ cup whipping cream
- sour cream and red pepper for garnishing

Patsy and her grandson

1. Cook bacon in Dutch oven, remove and drain grease, reserving 2 T.
2. Crumble bacon and set aside.
3. Saute' onion and carrots in bacon grease over medium-high heat until tender.
4. Add celery and apple to onion mixture and saute' 5 minutes.
5. Add garlic and saute' about 30 seconds.
6. Add butternut squash and chicken broth and bring to boil.
7. Reduce heat and simmer 20 minutes or until carrots are tender.
8. Process mixture in batches in a blender or food processor until smooth.
9. Return to Dutch oven and stir in lime juice and next 7 ingredients. Simmer 10-15 minutes or until thickened.
10. Top with crumbled bacon, sour cream and a sprinkle of red pepper.

Serves 8-10

PASTA FAGIOLI

from LEIGH

My very Irish friend Heidi O'Brien would often have us over for Pasta Fagioli (they lived 2 houses down) and my very Italian husband would INHALE it. You don't have to be Italian to love this soup - but you do have to make it in order to eat it (unless you are lucky enough to have a friendly neighbor like Heidi).

- 15 oz. can white northern beans
- 15 oz. can red kidney beans
- 14 oz. can double-strength beef broth
- 15 oz. can petite diced tomatoes
- 1 to 1½ cups macaroni pre-cooked (or other small pasta)
- 1 medium onion, diced
- 2 t. minced garlic, heaping
- 1 T. parsley
- 1 T. basil
- 1 t. oregano
- 2-3 T. olive oil
- 1 cube beef bouillon
- salt & pepper to taste

Heidi and Leigh...
good friends, good food, great life!

1. Sauté garlic, olive oil, onion and parsley until onion is tender.
2. Add all canned ingredients, plus seasonings, put lid on and simmer 30-45 minutes.
3. Cook macaroni in separate pot according to package directions, then let sit in water to soak about 15 minutes.
4. Drain noodles and add to soup.
5. Top individual servings with parmesan cheese.

Serves 6

The thing I love about soup
is that it usually comes
with a salad and a sandwich!
— SHELLEY

BLACK BEAN SOUP WITH ANDOUILLE SAUSAGE

from LEIGH

The great thing with this recipe is you can fix it in the Crockpot, go to work and it is ready when you get home. It makes the house smell so good!

- 2 fresh carrots, diced
- ½ cup of onion, diced
- 2 stalks of celery diced
- ½ Andouille sausage, cut in bite sizes
- 2 cans of black beans, drained
- 15 oz. can of diced tomatoes, not drained
- 1 cup of chicken broth
- 1 T. cumin
- 2 bay leaves
- 1 bunch of fresh cilantro chopped fine

1. Add all ingredients into Crockpot.
2. Cook 3 hrs. on high or 6 to 8 on low.
3. Remove bay leaves.

Serving suggestion: garnish by adding 2 cups lump crap meat on top.

Serves 6-8

COOKING CLASS #3

ROUX THE DAY: How (And Why) To Make A Roux

You may have noticed that recipes will sometimes instruct you to "make a roux." (See The Howards' Golden Potato Soup.) A roux is simply a mixture of butter and flour, which is used to thicken sauces, gravies and soups.

Follow these steps to make a delicious, golden brown roux:
1. Melt ½ stick of butter in a medium saucepan over medium-low heat. (for a darker brown roux, you would need to use cooking oil in place of the butter)
2. Add ¼ cup flour and stir constantly using whisk. (A whisk helps "break up" the ingredients.) The mixture will start to brown.
3. When roux reaches a light, golden brown color, it is ready to be used in your recipe.

To make a white sauce: whisk in 1 cup of milk and stir 'til smooth. White sauce is used in soufflés and as a base for sauces such as fettucine alfredo. (you can also add some sharp cheddar and drizzle over broccoli)

To make gravy: whisk in 14.5 oz. can of chicken broth or beef broth and ¼ to ½ cup of milk.

To make soup: add roux into soup and whisk until combined well with soup. It will take at least 20 minutes for the roux to thicken the soup.

BROCCOLI CHEESE SOUP

from DENISE

My friend Denise (whom I call Nee Nee) is an Air Force wife. She has lived all over the country and has been stationed with other incredible women who work together to raise their kids while the husbands are away serving our country. These courageous women form bonds like no other. Some nights they have potluck dinners just so they don't have to eat alone. Budgets are tight, so they might end up with just a soup and crackers night but they would fill up on love and friendship. This is one of their favorite soups to share.

- 10 oz. frozen chopped broccoli
- 1 medium onion, diced
- 3 cups water
- 1 can cream of celery soup
- 1 can cream of chicken soup
- 1 can cream of mushroom soup
- 2 cans cheddar cheese soup
- 2½ soup cans of milk
- 1 t. thyme
- 1 t. dill weed

1. Bring broccoli and onions to a boil in 3 cups of water.
2. Cook over medium heat for 5 minutes.
3. Add soups, milk, thyme and dill weed. Stir until the lumps are gone.
4. Cook for 5 minutes on medium. Do not allow to boil.

Serves 8

GREAT ADVICE FROM MY MOM!

DENISE: Mom says to make it easy for yourself. When you have people over, you want to enjoy the company. So, if it needs to be a paper plate sort of party, then do it. People aren't there for the china (although that is special sometimes, too), they are there to fellowship with you.

DAVID'S CHICKEN NOODLE SOUP

from SHELLEY

My father-in-law Phil used to own a restaurant called "The Trailside" in a little bitty town in Michigan called New Era. He tells us that one of the things he was famous for was his homemade soups. This is one that Phil taught my husband David to make and the secret, I believe, is in the stock base that they use. It's not like normal boullion cubes, rather, it's called "chicken base." We have found the same stuff his Dad used here in Nashville at a restaurant supply store. It's a chicken flavored paste-like substance. This is a deliciously basic chicken noodle soup that almost ends up being chicken and dumplings once it's reheated. When we tested this recipe for the cookbook, I helped Dave out a little with the chopping, but usually I just sit back and watch him make his magic in the kitchen! It doesn't happen often, but it's a beautiful sight when it does! (I left the recipe in David's words because I love the way that he describes the process!)

1. In your largest pot - boil 5 large boneless chicken breasts in 5 cups of water.
2. While boiling chicken prepare the following ingredients:
   - dice 1 large white onion (2 cups)
   - dice 1 package of celery - I use between 8-9 stalks (2 cups)
   - peal and dice 8-9 carrots (2 cups)
   - chop 2 cloves of garlic
   - 2 Bay Leaves

   (I put all of these ingredients in a bowl or on a plate as I prepare them so I can add them to the soup all at the same time).
3. When chicken is done - remove from water and let cool. Save the water the chicken was cooked in and use as the base for the soup.
4. Once the chicken has cooled, cut or shred the chicken into small pieces. I pull it apart to give long stringy pieces. I end up with about 4-5 cups of chicken.
5. Now it's time to add the chicken base - this is the key and something you will want to find. I use Knorr LeGout Chicken base. We get ours at a restaurant supply store and it is in a 16 oz. jar.
6. So, to the 5 cups of water (which has become broth), add ⅓ cup of the chicken base.
7. Then add all of your ingredients that you cut up earlier as well as the chicken.
8. Now add the following:
   - 1 t. salt
   - ½ T. pepper
   - 3 T. of parsley
9. Bring all of this to a rapid boil. Boil for 15-20 minutes to help break down the onions and garlic.
10. While you are boiling the soup, in a separate pot boil your noodles. I use a 16 oz. pack of extra wide egg noodles. When they are ready - strain and rinse and add to the soup.
11. Now reduce heat to low/simmer for 20-30 min.

Shelley and David

It's best the next day but you should have a few bowls right away while it is cooling!

Serves 12-14

SOUTHERN SALMON CHOWDER

from LEIGH

Nothing gets me more in the mood for fall than my mom's Salmon Stew. I still can't believe she talked us into eating this when we were kids. We LOVED it though, and we still empty the pot every time. However, this recipe has been altered since my sisters and I were kids, thanks to my husband Dana. He would say, "How can you think heated up milk with crackers tastes good?" Well, after the critique from her beloved son-in-law, Mom has enhanced it to include potatoes, celery and onion and spiced it up with dill and a touch of hot sauce. With these delicious additions to the recipe, it is now more of a chowder than a stew and Dana loves to eat it!

- 15 oz. can pink salmon w/ liquid
- ¼ cup celery chopped fine
- ¼ cup onion chopped fine
- 1 medium potato diced
- 5 oz. can evaporated milk
- 6 cups milk
- ½ t. thyme
- ½ t. basil
- salt to taste
- pepper to taste
- pinch crushed dill
- dash hot sauce
- 1 T. butter or margarine

1. Peel and chop vegetables.
2. Place in 4 quart Dutch oven and cover with water.
3. Simmer until tender.
4. While vegetables are simmering, de-bone salmon, saving liquid.
5. When vegetables are done, add evaporated milk, salmon with liquid and regular milk.
6. Season to taste with salt and pepper.
7. Add thyme, basil, hot sauce and butter.
8. Heat on medium heat to just before boiling point.
9. Serve with saltine crackers.

Serves 6-8

Leigh and her mom

ELEPHANT STEW

from POG

- 1 Elephant, medium size
- 2 Rabbits, optional
- salt and pepper
- brown gravy

1. Cut the elephant into bite size pieces.
2. Add enough brown gravy to cover.
3. Cook over fire about 4 weeks at 460 degrees.

This will serve 3800 people.
If more people are expected,
2 rabbits may be added.
Do this only in an emergency,
as most people do not like
hare in their stew.

*(No animals were harmed in the making of this cookbook.
POG does not advocate the poaching of endangered species!)*

WHITE TURKEY CHILI

from DENISE

After you've stuffed yourself all through the Christmas holidays, it's nice to lay back and have a lighter, healthier meal. This White Turkey Chili is the perfect solution. You can actually use 1% milk and the less sodium chicken broth to make it even healthier and not sacrifice the taste.

- 1 T. butter
- 1½ cups chopped onion
- ½ cup chopped celery
- ½ cup chopped red bell pepper
- 1 T. minced seeded jalepeno pepper
- 1 garlic clove, minced
- 3 cups cooked turkey or chicken
- 19 oz. can cannellini beans or other white beans, drained and divided
- Two 14.5 cans chicken broth
- 4 oz. can chopped green chiles
- 1 cup frozen corn
- 1½ t. ground cumin
- 1½ t. chili powder
- ¼ t. black pepper
- 1 cup low fat milk
- ½ cup fresh cilantro, chopped

menu SUGGESTIONS

CAJUN TWIST:
Black Bean Soup With Andouille
Mexican Cornbread (from Mexican Night chapter)
Turkey & Bacon Salad (from Salad chapter)

CHRISTMAS EVE CASUAL:
The Howards' Golden Potato Soup
Cornbread Casserole (from Side Dish chapter)
Crunchy Romaine Salad

SOUP & SANDWICH LUNCH:
David's Chicken Noodle
Open Face Ham Sandwiches (from Meat chapter)
Strawberry Pretzel Salad (from Salad chapter)

1. Melt butter in large Dutch oven over medium high heat.
2. Add onion, celery, red bell pepper, jalepeño pepper and garlic and saute' for 5 minutes.
3. Add turkey, 1½ cups beans, broth, chiles, corn, cumin, chili powder and black pepper and simmer for 15 minutes.
4. Mash remaining beans. Add mashed beans and milk to the turkey mixture.
5. Simmer uncovered 20 minutes or until mixture is thick, stirring frequently.
6. Stir in chopped cilantro.

Serves 8-10

CHAPTER FOUR

SO, YOU'RE IN THE MOOD FOR A
CASSEROLE

When we started pooling our recipes for this cookbook, we were amazed at how many casserole recipes we had. We couldn't believe we had enough to warrant a whole chapter dedicated to them. It suits us just perfectly because as far as we're concerned, casserole is love in a 9x13 baking dish! Whether we are pulling one out of the oven for our own families or packaging one up to take to a friend, nothing says "comfort" like a really good casserole.

BAKED ZITI

from LEIGH

There is a history of good cooking on both sides of my family. Mine is country cooking and my husband's side is Italian cooking. My dad owned several restaurants when I was growing up and Dana's Poppy owned several, too. The one most remembered by my husband is "The Three Caballero's." It was located in Poughkeepsie, NY and was owned by Poppy and two of his brothers.

North East folklore has it that "The Three Caballero's" restaurant is the original home of the "grinder" sandwich. So with all that Italian influence I must pay homage to the more Italian way of doing things. Trust me, to get any type of ingredient measurements was quite difficult. To quote my Italian Aunt Donna, "When you cook Italian, you do things by taste rather than a recipe. It's a little of this, a little of that and taste it to see if you need more. That's what Poppy taught us. So my recipe's are never exactly the same."

I must say this is a relaxing way to cook. Don't get caught up with measurements, only with taste!

- 1lb. ziti, cooked (according to package}
- 12 oz. jar of your favorite marinara sauce
- 8 oz. mozzarella cheese, shredded
- 1 cup grated parmesan cheese
- 8 oz. ricotta cheese
- 1 egg
- ¼ cup olive oil
- ¼ cup green bell peppers
- ¼ cup chopped onions
- 1 T. oregano
- 1 T. parsley
- 1 t. salt
- 1 t. pepper
- 1 t. garlic powder

"Three Cabellero's"... brothers Uncle Pat, Poppy and Uncle Gene Smmarco.

The restaurant menu

1. Preheat oven to 350.
2. Cook ziti in large pot and follow directions on package.
3. Put ¼ cup of olive oil in fry pan and sauté ¼ cup peppers, ¼ cup onions, 1 t. garlic powder, 1 t. oregano, 1 t. parsley, 1 tsp. salt, 1 tsp. pepper.
4. Cook until onions and peppers are soft.
5. Mix with marinara sauce.
6. Mix ricotta cheese and 1 egg in a big bowl.
7. Combine and mix with ½ of the cooked tomato sauce.
8. Mix in ziti.
9. Spread remaining tomato sauce in 9x13 baking dish
10. Place mixed ziti in baking dish and put the rest of sauce on top.
11. Pour grated parmesan cheese on top of the sauce.
12. Sprinkle shredded mozzarella cheese on top. (You may add more according to your desires!!!)
13. Bake for 30 minutes or until cheese is melted.
14. Let it stand for 10 to 15 minutes!! Enjoy!!!

Serves 8

MRS. SHAMBARGER'S POPPY SEED CHICKEN

from SHELLEY

When Denise and I were in college at Ouachita Baptist University in Arkansas, we were both in a girls' song and dance group called "The Ouachi-tones." The group was led by a wonderfully sweet lady named Mrs. Shambarger. She was somewhat of an icon at the college (and still is, even though she has been retired for years). I know, I know, "The Ouachi-tones"; it sounds funny, but it was THE group to be in and only a select few were chosen. Yes, I'm bragging. I did over-estimate my dancing abilities, however. On audition day, I knew I had a friend for life when Denise, who I had just met days before, helped me learn the dance steps for my audition. She was tirelessly patient with me, and trust me, I'm awful. Seriously, Denise is straight out of "Footloose" and I'm not kidding. She would KILL in "Dancing With the Stars," but that's another story! Anyway, we both made the group. I only lasted a year because I couldn't handle the stress of the choreography anymore. "Two left feet" doesn't begin to describe it. After I left the group, I didn't miss the dancing at all! The one thing I did miss was Mrs. Shambarger's Poppy Seed Chicken. Every year we would have a big Christmas party and this was always the main dish we were treated to. And I do mean "treated."

It is even possible to make friends out of your enemies with this one. I should know because there was a time when I wasn't sure if my neighbor Rob liked me, until their third child was born and I brought him and Kirsten this for dinner. I quickly became Rob's new best friend, and now he is in my kitchen almost every day to see what I'm cookin'.

- 5 cups cooked, chopped chicken breast (approx. 4 lg. breasts = 5 cups)
- 32 oz. sour cream
- 2 cans cream of mushroom soup
- 4 sleeves of buttery crackers, crushed
- 2 sticks butter (melted)
- 3 T. poppy seeds
- 6 cups cooked white rice

1. Preheat oven to 350.
2. Grease 9x13 casserole dish.
3. Combine chicken, sour cream and mushroom soup until mixed thoroughly. (set aside)
4. In separate bowl combine crackers, butter and poppy seeds until mixed thoroughly.
5. Layer half of chicken mixture in bottom of dish.
6. Top with half of the cracker mixture.
7. Repeat layers.
8. Bake for 40 minutes or until hot and bubbly.

Serve over white rice.

Serves 10-12

DENISE
SHELLEY

Mrs. Shambarger and her Ouachi-tones, circa 1988

CHICKEN AND DRESSING CASSEROLE

from SHELLEY

The old saying, "There's no place like home" couldn't be more true. I loved growing up in Little Rock and for the most part my entire family still lives there. The road there from Nashville isn't too long. We can usually drive it in five or six hours, so we try to get there for visits as much as we can. You can always count on my mom to have delicious food prepared for "the kids". She especially likes to take care of her adopted "sons," my husband David and my brother-in-law, Kyle. She never forgets anything they happen to mention liking, so you can be sure her pantry is stocked with Ruffles and there is always onion dip and an endless supply of Mountain Dew™ in the fridge. One meal I remember her making one Thursday night as we drove into town for a visit was this Chicken and Dressing casserole. I actually remember that she kept it warm in the Crockpot for us, which actually worked very well. I think she adapted this from an old Southern Living recipe awhile back. I've gotten some great recipes from that magazine over the years and a yearly subscription is often tucked into our stocking by Santa.

(Make night before and refrigerate overnight)

- 4 large boneless, skinless chicken breasts
- 1 can cream of chicken soup
- 1 can cream of mushroom soup
- One 8 oz pkg. herb-seasoned stuffing mix
- ½ cup butter or margarine, melted

1. Cook chicken in boiling water 'til tender.
2. Remove chicken from broth. Strain broth, reserving 2⅔ cups.
3. Cut meat into small pieces. Set aside.
4. Combine chicken soup with half the broth; mix well and set aside.
5. Combine mushroom soup with remaining broth; mix well and set aside.
6. Combine stuffing mix and butter; reserve ¼ cup for garnish.
7. Spoon half of remaining stuffing mixture in lightly greased 9x13 inch baking dish; top with half the chicken.
8. Cover with chicken soup mixture; repeat layers.
9. Pour mushroom soup over layers; sprinkle with reserved stuffing mixture.
10. Cover and refrigerate overnight.
11. Remove casserole from refrigerator 15 minutes before baking.
12. Uncover and bake at 350 for 30-45 minutes.

Serves 8

COOKING CLASS #4

COOKED, DICED CHICKEN BREAST:
When a recipe calls for diced chicken breast:
1. Place chicken breasts, frozen or fresh, in medium sauce pan (1 average size breast = approximately 1 cup diced).
2. Barely cover chicken with water, then put lid on the pan and bring to a boil over high heat.
3. Turn heat down to low and simmer (which means "to cook just below the boiling point") for 15-20 minutes.
4. Cut into chicken to see if it's done. Chicken should be white all the way through.

If you are really pressed for time, buy the already prepared rotisserie chicken from the grocery store. Dice it up and it's ready to go in a casserole!

JANICE'S ITALIAN DELIGHT

from DENISE

This was a standard casserole that we had a lot around my house. I loved it even more as a leftover after basketball practice or as an afternoon snack. It's easy and most of the time you have the ingredients in your pantry when you don't have anything else to make for dinner.

- 1 lb. ground beef
- 1 small or medium onion
- 1 T. chili powder
- garlic salt to taste
- 12 oz. package of egg noodles
- 16 oz. can of tomato sauce
- 1 small can of sweet corn, drained
- 1½ cups shredded cheddar cheese

1. Preheat oven to 350.
2. While cooking noodles as directed on package, brown the hamburger meat.
3. Add onion to the meat and cook 'til onions are done, then drain.
4. Add tomato sauce, chili powder and garlic salt to meat.
5. Simmer for 5 minutes.
6. Mix meat mixture with cooked noodles and corn in a 9x13 casserole pan.
7. Bake for 30 to 35 min.
8. Top with cheese and put back in the oven for the cheese to melt, about 5 minutes.

My true delight... my family!

OPTIONAL:
For a little taste of Mexico, you can add a little more chili powder and mix it with crushed tortilla chips instead of noodles. (We called it Taco Pie.)

Serves 6-8

JULIE'S EASY CHICKEN PIE

from SHELLEY

When my daughter was little, one of maybe five things she actually enjoyed for dinner was chicken pot pie. The thing is, I always just got the pre-packaged frozen variety. (By the way, how in the world are there 8,000 calories in those little store-bought frozen pot pies?? I cannot figure that one out!) As I've gotten older and have a little more time, I have tried as much as I can to trade in the frozen quick dinner options for the real thing. This recipe is one that my good friend Julie created. It is a relatively simple, but very delicious, version of a standard homemade chicken pot pie. I know your family will love it just as much as mine does.

- 1 box Pillsbury refrigerated pie dough (you will use both crusts)
- 1 12 oz. can of chicken breast (drained) (or you can boil and dice 2 chicken breasts)
- 1 box frozen broccoli, cauliflower & carrots in cheese sauce (cooked)
- ½ cup frozen peas
- ¼ cup butter
- ½ cup flour
- 1 cup chicken broth
- ¾ cup milk

1. Preheat oven to 350.
2. Roll one pie crust into a pie plate and prick all over with fork.
3. Bake at 350 for 10 minutes.
4. Remove from oven and spread chicken breast over crust.
5. Spread veggies in cheese sauce over chicken.
6. Sprinkle frozen peas on top and set aside.
7. In large, nonstick skillet melt butter over med-hi heat.
8. Add flour and stir with whisk until combined well with butter and starting to brown.
9. Add chicken broth and whisk until thickened.
10. Add milk and keep whisking for about 3 minutes or until good "sauce" consistency.
11. Pour over ingredients in pie plate.
12. Lay second crust on top and prick top several times with fork.
13. Bake for 25 minutes or until top is golden brown.

Serves 6

STUFFED EGGPLANT

from LEIGH

My husband Dana LOVES eggplant. His Nanny Sammarco made stuffed eggplant when he was growing up and I have not had the courage to fix it myself. I figure, why ruin a good thing? Plus, I don't really know how to find a good eggplant. It is an Italian art form to know how to choose the perfect eggplant. Luckily, we still enjoy this dish when we visit New York because Aunt Donna now makes them. Give 'em a try!

- 6 small Italian eggplants washed, cut in half length-wise and flesh scooped out and diced
- 1 onion, diced
- 1 tomato, diced
- 1 T. fresh parsley, snipped
- 1 T. fresh basil, snipped
- salt and pepper to taste
- 1 cup of ricotta cheese
- ½ cup bread crumbs
- ½ cup of grated parmesan cheese
- 2 eggs slightly beaten
- 3 T. olive oil, divided use

My Italian family - Tina/mother in law, Uncle Val, Aunt Donna and Dana's grandmother "Nanny" Mary

1. Preheat oven to 350.
2. Arrange the eggplant halves in a 9x13 baking dish that has 1 T. olive oil on the bottom.
3. Sauté the onions and the diced eggplant in 2 T. olive oil until soft.
4. Add the diced tomatoes and cook a few minutes longer.
5. Take off the stove to cool.
6. In a bowl mix the eggs, ricotta, and seasonings.
7. Mix in the grated cheese and bread crumbs.
8. Stuff the eggplant shells with cheese mixture.
9. Cover the dish with aluminum foil and bake for 45 minutes.
10. Uncover and bake for another 15 minutes. Enjoy!!! (They are even good cold.)

Serves 6-8

The great thing about casseroles is that you can make them ahead of time, clean the kitchen and still have the wonderful smell in the air for your company!

— LEIGH

SAUSAGE, CHICKEN & CRANBERRY CASSEROLE

from SHELLEY

From the same neighbor, Kathy, who brought you the Onion Souffle' recipe in the appetizer section comes this incredible casserole. Trust me when I say it is DELISH!! It's a wonderful dish to ring in the fall season. Nashville is such a small town when it comes down to it and the wonderful girl, Julie, who helped us put this cookbook together has a sister named Betsy who loves to cook as much as we do. Turns out, Betsy is great friends with Kathy and got this recipe from her. I guess you could say I got this one by two degrees of separation! But I'm not bitter that Kathy has never made it for me...not at all...really...I'm not...

- 5 or 6 pieces of chicken breast, cooked and diced
- 1 lb. sausage with sage, cooked and drained
- 1 box wild rice, cooked
- 1 can whole cranberries
- 1 can cream of mushroom soup
- 2 cups sharp cheddar cheese, grated
- ¾ cup slivered almonds, toasted

1. Preheat oven to 400.
2. Combine all ingredients, mix well.
3. Pour into greased 9x13 baking dish.
4. Bake for 30 minutes.

Serves 6-8

a quick POINT

Tips on taking meals to people:

1. Try to stay away from traditional pasta dishes, such as spaghetti and lasagna. People tend to get a lot of those.
2. Take the main entrée and at least 2 sides, such as salad and bread or green bean bundles and potato casserole.
3. Don't forget dessert! It doesn't even have to be "from scratch". Oatmeal/Cranberry/Walnut "break and bake" cookies in the refrigerated section are really good and they taste homemade!
4. Label all containers with the name of the food it contains and the cooking directions. All containers should be disposable.
5. Get in and get out! If someone is recovering from surgery or has just had a baby, try to limit your visit to no more than 20 to 30 minutes.

RANDI'S VEGETABLE LASAGNA

from DENISE

Having a close circle of friends provides many wonderful things in your life. Good advice, prayer warriors, a shoulder to cry on and someone to celebrate with you are just a few. Lately, though, we have been sharing recipes! This recipe comes from my friend Randi. She makes this wonderful Veggie Lasagna when someone has a baby or has had surgery. We have all been blessed by this dish at one time or another and now we ALL make it!

- 12 oz. lasagna noodles, cooked
- 1½ cup store-bought pesto sauce
- 1 cup shredded parmesan cheese (for topping)

Cheese mixture: combine below ingredients and set aside
- 2 cups of ricotta cheese
- ¾ cup grated parmesan
- ¾ cup grated romano
- 1 cup shredded mozzarella
- ½ cup snipped parsley
- 1 beaten egg yolk

Vegetable mixture:
- ½ onion
- 2 medium zucchini (sliced)
- 2 medium yellow squash (sliced)
- 16 oz. crimini mushrooms
- 4 oz. black olives (sliced)
Above are sautéed together in 2 T. butter or olive oil

Add to vegetable mixture and continue sautéing:
- 1 t. Italian seasoning
- ½ t. dried marjoram
- 2 cloves garlic, pressed
- salt and pepper to taste

Randi and her friends at the camp she and her husband own

1. Preheat oven to 350.
2. In 9x13 casserole dish, layer noodles, cheese mixture, pesto sauce and veggie mixture.
3. Repeat 2 or 3 more times. (3 or 4 layers total)
4. Top the lasagna with 1 cup of shredded parmesan cheese.

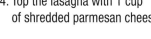

Serves 8-10

CHICKEN ROLL-UPS

from DENISE

In our last year of college, Shelley and I were roommates with another one of our best friends named Cathy. We lived in a garage apartment owned by one of the sweetest families in the world, the Hargetts. Mrs. Hargett was like our Mom away from home. She was always making little treats or wonderful meals that we would get to enjoy when her son Chuck (also one of our best friends) came home. For Chuck's birthday dinner that year, he wanted his mom to make Chicken Roll-Ups. I thought they were soooo good. When I found out how easy they were, this dish became a staple at my house. I'm all about the shortcuts, so here ya go....

- 1 can of 8 refrigerated crescent rolls
- 10 oz. can chunk white chicken (or you can cook your own chicken – 1 or 2 pieces, diced)
- 1 can cream of chicken soup (optional 2 cans for a creamier taste)
- 2 ½ cups shredded cheddar cheese – divided use
- Salt and pepper to taste

1. Pre-heat oven to 350.
2. Spread out some foil and lay out the crescent rolls.
3. In each roll put:
   A little chicken
   2 T. shredded cheese
   salt and pepper
4. Roll them up and put in deep dish.
5. Whip cream of chicken soup with 1 can water, or simply use 2 cans without water for a creamier taste (since its thicker, you'll have to spread it with a spoon)
6. Pour soup around the rolls.
7. Cook for 30 minutes.
8. Sprinkle with ½ cup cheese and cook for 5 or 10 more minutes until cheese is melted.

Serve over a bed of rice.

Serves 6-8

A rare photo of Mrs. Hargett (she hated being photographed), and Chuck, who also designed this cookbook

CINDY'S DIVINE DIVAN

from LEIGH

Our baby girl had been home from the hospital for about two months. I was still very tired and ALWAYS hungry. When my best friend from college came to visit, she took great care of me and our little "punkin." Cindy was wonderful, making meals, letting me sleep, etc. This one particular evening she prepared Chicken Divan for dinner. I had no idea what "Chicken Divan" was and I certainly didn't know what curry was, but when she told me, "It's the curry that makes this dish so fantastic," I realized I might be addicted. Now I always say, "You can never have too much curry!" I left the table completely satisfied and thrilled that my spice rack embraced a new and very delicious addition - curry!

Leigh, before Darby was born, and Cindy. She has been the greatest friend!

- 4 chicken breasts
- 1 can cream of chicken soup
- 1- 2 T. of fresh squeezed lemon juice
- 1 cup mayonnaise (my favorite is Dukes)
- 2 cups sharp cheddar cheese, grated (divided use)
- curry powder to taste (I suggest 2 t.)
- 12 oz. bag of frozen broccoli cooked, drained and chopped

1. Preheat oven to 350.
2. Boil chicken breasts and cut into bite size pieces.
3. Mix all ingredients. (minus the broccoli and 1 cup of cheese)
4. In 9x13 baking dish add broccoli to bottom and add mixture on top of broccoli.
5. Add 1 cup shredded cheese to top of mixture.
6. Bake for 45-60 minutes

Serves 4-6

SPICY CHICKEN SPAGHETTI

from SHELLEY

I know there are a lot of Chicken Spaghetti recipes floating around out there, but this is my all time favorite! The secret is boiling the noodles IN the chicken broth, not to mention the shredded Velveeta! It makes a TON, so take some to your neighbors!

- 16 oz. package of spaghetti
- 5 cups of boiled chicken, chopped
- 1 can cream of mushroom soup
- 1 can cream of chicken soup
- 1 onion, chopped
- ½ green pepper, chopped
- 1 stick of butter plus one additional T.
- 2 cups shredded Velveeta
- 1 can original Ro-tel tomatoes
- 1 sleeve of buttery crackers

1. Preheat oven to 350.
2. Boil chicken until cooked through.
3. Remove chicken from pan, reserving broth.
4. Cool chicken and boil spaghetti in reserved chicken broth according to package directions.
5. While spaghetti is cooking, saute' chopped onion and green pepper 'til tender in one T. of butter.
6. Drain spaghetti and mix with chicken, soups, sautéed onion, green pepper and Ro-tel.
7. Spoon into a greased 9x13 pan.
8. Melt remaining stick of butter.
9. Crush crackers finely and mix with butter.
10. Top spaghetti with cracker mixture and bake until brown and bubbly, about 40 minutes.

Serves 10-12

CROCKPOT STEAK STROGANOFF

from DENISE

We all live extremely busy lives. I can't quite figure out how my mom could always start dinner and have it on the table during the "witching" hour, as I like to call it. Homework is trying to get finished, kids are grumpy and hungry, Mom is grumpy and hungry, there is a practice or lesson that they need to get to after dinner and you've been gone all day with errands or meetings and carpool. Whew! Well, the Crockpot has become my short cut for this kind of day. All you have to do is think ahead just a little bit by making sure you have your ingredients in the fridge to prepare that morning. It saves me from turning into the "Wicked Witch!"

- 2 T. flour
- ½ t. garlic powder
- ½ t. pepper
- ¼ t. paprika
- 1 ¾ lb. boneless beef round steak
- 1 can cream of mushroom soup
- ½ cup water
- 1 envelope dried onion soup mix
- 9 oz. jar sliced mushrooms, drained
- ½ cup sour cream
- 1 T. minced fresh parsley

1. Combine flour, garlic powder, pepper, and paprika in crockpot.
2. Cut meat into 1½ x ½ inch strips.
3. Place in flour mixture and toss until meat is well coated.
4. Add meat to crockpot.
5. Add mushroom soup, water and soup mix. Stir until well blended.
6. Cover. Cook on high 3-3½ hours, or low 6-7 hours.
7. Stir in mushrooms, sour cream, and parsley. Cover and cook on high 10 -15 minutes, or until heated through.
8. Serve over rice or wide egg noodles.

Serves 6-8

CREAMY GROUND BEEF & CORN CASSEROLE

from SHELLEY

This is a casserole that my mother used to make a lot. For some odd reason, I NEVER liked it growing up. I have no idea why. I think it was the French fried onion rings or maybe the pimentos but now my palate is quite refined. French fried onion rings, bring them on! This really does have a great flavor, I mean, can you think of anything that has a block of cream cheese in it that ISN'T good?? Just sayin'...

- 1 lb. ground beef
- ½ cup chopped onions
- 8 oz. cream cheese
- 1 can cream of mushroom soup
- 15 oz. can corn, partially drained
- 2 oz. jar chopped pimento
- 1 tsp. salt
- Dash of pepper
- 1 small can French fried onion rings

1. Preheat oven to 375.
2. Brown beef and onions in large skillet; drain any grease.
3. In same skillet, with beef mixture, melt in cream cheese and add soup.
4. Stir in corn (partially drained).
5. Add pimentos and salt and pepper.
6. Put in greased 2-quart casserole dish.
7. Bake for about 20 minutes.
8. Place French fried onion rings on top and bake an additional 5-10 minutes.

Serves 6-8

menu SUGGESTIONS

CHRISTMAS LUNCHEON:
Sausage, Chicken & Cranberry Casserole, Amy Grant's Red & Green Romaine Salad (from Salad chapter), Quick Herbed Dill Rolls (from Side Dish chapter), Pecan Pie and Pumpkin Pie (from Dessert Chapter)

ITALIAN FEAST:
Baked Ziti, Stuffed Eggplant, Super Wilted Salad (from Salad Chapter), French bread (store-bought - slice, spread with butter and garlic salt and bake at 400 til crusty and brown) and Easy Breezy Chocolate Bundt (from Dessert chapter)

COMFORT FOOD:
Chicken Roll-ups served with rice, Lucy's Sweet & Sour Green Beans (from Side Dish chapter) and Chocolate Pie (from Dessert chapter)

PAIGE'S BUTTERNUT SQUASH LASAGNA

from DENISE

My friend Paige also happens to be my personal trainer. She only comes once a week and can't stop my bad habit of eating junk food. Anyway, she and her husband are really good cooks. One night we sang for a private dinner party and Paige and her husband catered the dinner for the people there. We got to sit in the kitchen and eat some of the leftovers before it was time to sing. One of the things they cooked was this butternut squash lasagna. It was incredible. I called her up and told her that we wanted to put this recipe in the cookbook for sure. My biggest tip is this: don't eat it the night before your trainer comes to work you out!

- 3 pounds butternut squash, peeled, seeded, and cut into ¼ to ½ inch slices
- 3 T. olive oil
- ½ t. salt
- ¼ cup butter
- 6 cloves garlic, minced
- ¼ cup all purpose flour
- ½ t. salt
- 4 cups milk
- 1 T. snipped fresh parsley
- 9 "no boil" lasagna noodles
- 1⅓ cups finely shredded parmesan cheese
- 1 cup whipping cream

Paige and Denise

Squash:
1. Preheat oven to 425.
2. Lightly grease a 15x10x1 baking pan.
3. Place squash in the prepared baking pan.
4. Add oil and ½ t. salt, toss gently to coat. Spread an even layer.
5. Roast uncovered for 25 to 30 min. or until squash is tender, stirring once.
6. Reduce oven temp to 375 degrees.

Sauce:
7. Meanwhile, for sauce; in large saucepan, heat butter over med-heat.
8. Add garlic; cook and stir for 1 min.
9. Stir in flour and ½ t. salt.
10. Gradually stir in milk.
11. Cook and stir until thickened and bubbly.

12. Stir in squash and rosemary.
13. Lightly grease a 9x13 baking dish.

Assembly:
14. To assemble, spread about 1 cup of the sauce in the prepared baking dish.
15. Layer 3 noodles in dish.
16. Spread with 1/3 of remaining sauce.
17. Sprinkle with 1/3 cup of the Parmesan cheese.
18. Repeat layering of noodles, sauce and Parmesan cheese two more times.
19. Pour whipping cream evenly over layers in the dish.
20. Sprinkle with remaining Parmesan cheese.
21. Cover dish with foil. Bake for 40 min.
22. Uncover and bake about 10 min more until edges are bubbly and top is lightly browned.
23. Let stand for 10 min before serving.

(Optional - You can also add chopped pecans as a topping in the last 10 min of baking.)

Serves 10-12

CHAPTER FIVE

SO, WE'RE NOT VEGETARIANS, Y'ALL!
MEAT

We are meat eaters, so we have given you an assortment of recipes to try out for that main entrée. Whether it's an elegant dinner party or a casual, family meal, meat is the star of the show and will set the tone for the rest of the menu. These recipes will make you a star, too!

MOM'S OKLAHOMA BARBECUE BRISKET

from DENISE

I grew up in Oklahoma and our diet consisted of meat and potatoes. Barbecue brisket is one of my all time favorite meats. There are many ways to cook brisket. You can grill it, smoke it, bake it and the list goes on, but I'm a simple cook and this is what works for me. I don't follow exact measurements, so I'll try my best to tell you how I do it.
(NOTE: Don't make the same mistake that I made when I was a newlywed trying to impress my sweet husband with a home cooked meal. Do NOT buy "corned-beef!"
I cooked it and cooked it and couldn't understand why in the world the meat was still red! Just buy a regular brisket.)

- 2½ to 3 lb beef brisket
- salt and pepper
- ¼ stick butter
- Worcestershire sauce
- Your favorite barbecue sauce (mine is Head Country from Ponca City, OK. You can order it online.)

Denise and her mom

1. Preheat oven to 250.
2. Lay brisket in a large casserole pan and take a fork and poke each side of the meat several times.
3. Spread 1 T. butter over one side of the brisket and then shake salt and pepper over it.
4. Flip the meat and repeat the butter and salt.
5. Lay the brisket in the pan with the fatty side on top.
6. Pour a liberal amount of Worcestershire sauce all over the top of the brisket.
7. Cover pan with foil and bake for about 6 hours. Take brisket out and drain off the juice (Note: You might want to cut off some of the fat and throw it away.)
8. Spread the barbecue sauce on top of the brisket and put back in the oven for another 20 min uncovered until sauce thickens on the brisket.
9. Take out and slice against the grain of the meat.

Serves 8-10

MARINATED GRILLED FLANK STEAK

from SHELLEY

I remember the first time I ever ate this steak. It was at Julie's house (yes, the girl whose name is on the front of this cookbook) and I just thought it was the most flavorful meat I had ever eaten. I anxiously got the recipe from her mom and I couldn't wait to cook it at home. The best part was that my husband LOVED it just as much as I did and he's not one to get overly excited about food. (I guess opposites DO attract.) So, I decided to cook it for dinner one night for some good friends who had just moved to Nashville from Texas. I built the steak up to them and told them they were just going to DIE when they tasted how good it was. Well, I marinated it overnight and David cooked it perfectly on the grill. The only problem was, it just didn't taste anything like Julie's. I mean, it just tasted like plain ol' meat. I KNEW I had followed the marinade recipe, but even David admitted it was kinda "whatever". Well, I finally figured out the problem was in my "scoring" technique. In order for the meat to really absorb the flavor of the marinade, you have to "score" it. The translation that I did not know is: "beat it, cut it, rip it into a bloodier pulp than it already is." Therein lies the secret to flavorful flank steak. Julie's mom, "T.," basically told me to score the meat beyond all recognition! So, this is a great recipe if you are feeling vengeful or angry. You can just take your frustration out on the meat and it'll just make it better! By the way, our company was very gracious and didn't seem to mind the flavorless hunk of meat I set before them. Score, people! Score with all your might!

- Two 1 – 1½ lb. flank steaks
- 1 clove garlic
- 1 t. salt
- 1 T. vegetable oil
- 1 T. ketchup or tomato paste
- 3 T. soy sauce
- ½ t. oregano
- ½ t. pepper

1. Place whole clove garlic and salt in shallow bowl.
2. Mash the garlic into the salt with a fork.
3. Add the rest of the ingredients and mix well.
4. Lay flank steak on a large sheet of plastic wrap.
5. Score meat on both sides: take a sharp knife and make diagonal cuts across the top going in both directions (this will create "diamond" shapes on steak):
6. Spread the marinade on steaks, on both sides.
7. Wrap the steaks snugly in plastic wrap and place in baking dish or plastic zip bag and refrigerate overnight (or at least 6 hours).
8. Take steaks out of the refrigerator 15 minutes before grilling.
9. Heat up grill and throw the steaks on!

Julie's husband, Mark, says to remember the 5 minute rule for grilling perfect flank steak:
set your timer and turn the meat every 5 minutes. 15 minutes total should do it for steak cooked to "medium."

Serves 6-8

ONION POCKET BURGERS

from SHELLEY

My mom says she got this recipe years ago when she and my dad got their first gas grill. She wants me to tell you it's especially great when sweet Vidalia onions are in season!

- 1 cup ketchup
- 1 T. Worcestershire sauce
- 1 T. mustard
- 1 T. brown sugar
- ½ t. celery seed
- 3 large onions, cut in half crosswise
- 1½ lbs. lean ground beef
- 1 egg, slightly beaten
- ⅓ cup chopped green pepper
- 1½ t. salt
- ⅛ t. pepper
- Heavy duty aluminum foil

1. Combine first 5 ingredients to make a sauce; set aside.
2. Scoop out centers (several layers) of onions.
3. Place each onion half on an 18 in. square of aluminum foil.
4. In large bowl, combine ground beef, egg, green pepper, salt, pepper and ¾ cup of sauce.
5. Shape meat mixture into 6 balls and place in each onion half.
6. Pour remaining sauce over each onion.
7. Wrap up each square so sauce won't leak out.
8. Grill over indirect heat on medium for about 50-60 minutes or 'til done.

Serves 6

COOKINGCLASS #5

GREAT GRILLING TIPS: I have to admit shortly after Shelley and I were married I began to feel stressed whenever she would say we were having company over and I was responsible for picking out and grilling the steaks. What if I ruin the steak? What if I burn it? What if it's cold in the middle?

So, I started to look for grilling shows on the Food Channel to make sure I knew what I was doing. One day around Fourth of July weekend, I saw that our local TV noonday show was having a segment about how to grill steaks using a gas grill. Here is what I learned:

1. Basically they said to heat the grill as hot as it can get.
2. Make sure your steak is marinated the way you like it. (We always use Allegro marinade.)
3. Then, using tongs, put the steak on the grill and leave it for 2 minutes.
4. Next, lift and turn it 90 degrees - this will give you the criss cross grill marks on the steak as well as sear in the juices.
5. Leave it for another 3 minutes - then flip it. Repeat the process on the other side - waiting 2 minutes then rotating it 90 degrees.
6. Leave it on for another 3 minutes.
7. With the grill marks on both sides and a total cook time of 10 minutes, if your steak is not the temperature you want (it is probably rare at this point depending on the thickness) - move it to the top shelf to slow cook away from the direct heat until it is to your liking.

This procedure has helped me to be more confident when grilling steaks. Hopefully it will help you as well.

GUEST INSTRUCTOR
DAVID BREEN

GRANDDADDY'S FRIED CUBE STEAK

from LEIGH

Sunday "dinner" was a family tradition for many years (we didn't call it lunch back then even though it was served at 1 pm, immediately after church service). When everyone was there, we had about 20 people to feed. It was always served buffet style on the kitchen bar and there was always a separate table for us grandkids. Can you believe we always got served first? (What snotty nosed brats!) The adults and teenagers had to scramble for seats at the kitchen table, dining room table and card tables set up on the glassed in front porch. The last one in line got the lone seat at the kitchen bar.

Even when grandmother was alive, granddaddy seemed to be in charge of cooking Sunday dinner. The entrees were always the same, but they rotated. We would have fried chicken the first Sunday, pot roast the second, baked ham the third and everyone's favorite, fried cube steak, on the fourth Sunday. On the rare fifth Sunday of a month it was pork chops, fried of course. (My personal aside: How are we all still alive and relatively healthy after eating this every Sunday? Everything was fried, including squash and okra for sides!)

Granddaddy cooked the cubed steak before he left home for Sunday school and left it in a warm oven for over 2 hours while we were at church. My Aunt Wren remembers Granddaddy saying that leaving it in the warm oven was the secret to it being so tender. I think we also loved this Sunday dinner so much because of the rice and browned milk gravy (made from the pan drippings) that was always served with it.

Today, we all aim to be healthier in our eating and diets, but fried cubed steak would still be my first choice for a special family meal, even over filet mignon!

- 2 lbs. cube steak
- ½ t. salt
- ¼ t. pepper
- ½ cup flour
- 3-4 T. vegetable oil

1. Preheat oven to 150.
2. Cut cube steak into desired pieces.
3. Combine flour, salt and pepper in a shallow bowl and mix well.
4. Dip each piece of meat into flour mixture and cover well.
5. Heat oil in large frying pan on medium high.
6. Place meat in frying pan and turn heat down to medium low.
7. Brown meat on both sides, until cooked all the way through.
8. Place meat in pan and seal with aluminum foil.
9. Place in oven and go to church. (just kidding!)
10. Place in oven for 2 hours.

Steak will be piping hot and tender!

Serves 6-8

-Leigh and Aunt Wren

AMY GRANT'S POT ROAST

(We asked Amy Grant to submit something yummy for our cookbook and she was so sweet to oblige. When she emailed this recipe to us through her manager, she said, "Here's the recipe...I hope they print it as it is..." Well, when Amy talks, we listen. So, here it is, straight from Amy to you! There isn't a sweeter person in the world! Thanks, Amy, for this wonderful contribution!)

from AMY

A speckled, blue enamel roasting pan that used to belong to Vince's grandmother now sits in my pantry. That has been reason enough for me to perfect my pot roast recipe. Thanks to my mother-in-law, Jerene, who taught me to sear the beef before putting it in the roaster, I think I've got a pretty good thing going.

Before you get overwhelmed by the portion size, let me say, I like to cook BIG meals; partly, because I love leftovers, but mostly because that gives me the chance to pack up a take-home meal for whoever might drop by. This is a great dish to make on a day I know I'll be staying home.

Ingredients:
(I'm going to put my portion sizes here, but feel free to do less and split the amounts of everything.)
• 2 or 3 Chuck Roasts (enough to fill the pan from end to end in a single layer, usually about 7 lbs of meat)
• Olive oil (just enough for a quick splash in the skillets before I sear the roasts)
• 4 or 5 onions (cut in big chunks)
• Six 14 oz. cans of beef broth
• Montreal Steak Seasoning
• Fresh garlic (I use a spoonful of the kind that comes in a jar)
• 8 oz. red wine (more or less)
• Salt and Pepper
• 1 can cream of mushroom soup
• Maple syrup (just a drizzle)
• Bag of carrots
• Bag of new potatoes

DO NOT SHOWER BEFORE YOU START THIS PROCESS, because you will definitely need one when you are finished.

Vince and his mother Jerene

Now the fun begins:
1. Put two large skillets on the stove, burners all the way on high.
2. Unwrap the meat and cover LIBERALLY with Montreal Steak Seasoning
3. Drizzle olive oil into the skillets a minute before the meat is laid in.

(cont. next page...)

4. Sear the beef. (I almost blacken it.)
5. While the meat is searing, prepare the roasting pan by quartering the onions and filling the bottom of the pan. (Vince HATES onions, but doesn't mind these because they cook away to nothing and leave a natural sweetness)
6. Lay the seared meat on top of the onions and add enough beef broth to partially cover the chuck roasts (in my roaster it takes 4 cans)
7. Stir in garlic and wine.
8. Salt and pepper to taste (this tastes pretty bad, because nothing is blended, but the salt and pepper value is important because it will cook into the meat. Make the salt level taste good to you.)
9. Speaking of salt and pepper, I keep a bowl of finely ground kosher salt and black pepper (3:1 ratio) on my kitchen counter at all times. Rather than measure in spoons, I use big finger pinches as a measure. This requires a lot of tasting.
10. Place roasting pan in 400 degree oven. Cook for about 4 hours checking liquid levels every hour or so.
11. When meat pulls apart easily add last two cans of beef broth, one can of cream of mushroom soup and a drizzle of maple syrup (maybe 3 Tablespoons). Blend in the pot.
12. Then add carrots and potatoes: as many as the pot will hold, spooning liquid over veggies
13. Cook for another hour (or until potatoes are easily pierced with a fork) and SERVE!

Amy and Vince

SWEET & SPICY ASIAN CHICKEN

from DENISE

My dear friend Karri is not only a good cook, but has passed her talents down to her youngest son, Samuel. He's 15 years old and has a knack for cooking. I asked him what his favorite recipe was and this is the one he sent. I'm so sure! It's way more complicated than I would dare attempt. I don't even know what orange zest and mirin is. He assures me that it is not as hard as it looks. It's hard to believe that the same little boy who used to call me "Miss-ter Neece" (supposed to be Miss Denise) is making this unique dish. He will probably have his own TV show some day! You go, Sam!

- 2 T. orange zest
- 1 cup canned pineapple juice
- 2 cups fresh orange juice
- 2 T. minced garlic
- 2 T. minced green onions
- 1 T. sesame oil
- ½ cup soy sauce
- ½ cup mirin (a japanese sweet cooking wine)
- 1 cup sugar
- ½ t. crushed red pepper
- 2 quarts peanut oil
- 8 boneless skinless chicken breasts (cut into strips or nugget size)
- 2 cups cornstarch
- 4 T. Emeril's Original Essence (look in spice section of grocery store)
- 1 cup cilantro
- 1 cup toasted sesame seeds

Sam and Denise

1. Combine: Orange juice, pineapple juice, orange zest, garlic, ginger, green onions, sesame oil, soy sauce, mirin, sugar, and red pepper in large skillet set over med-high heat.
2. Bring to a boil, stirring occasionally, until sugar is dissolved and the liquid has reduced to a thick syrup, 18 to 20 min.
3. Place oil in pot and heat to 375.
4. Place chicken strips in a large bowl.
5. In a small bowl, season the cornstarch with essence.
6. Place the seasoned cornstarch in a gallon bag and put chicken pieces in batches.
7. Shake and place in hot oil.
8. Fry chicken 6 to 8 min.
9. Remove and season lightly with salt.
10. Preheat oven to 275 degrees.
11. Spoon sauce over chicken and toss to coat.
12. Sprinkle chicken with cilantro and sesame seeds.
13. Keep warm in oven till guests arrive and serve with steamed rice.

Serves 8
(Half the recipe very easily for 4 chicken breasts)

SIMPLE FLOUNDER

from LEIGH

I absolutely could not wait to eat this growing up. It was one of my favorite childhood meals. Whether I was in the den watching TV, or in my bedroom, I could smell it from afar. The butter and garlic filled up our little ranch house. No need to call me to the table, I was ready and waiting.

- 4 or 5 flounder fillets (1 lb.)
- 1 stick butter
- 3 T. lemon juice
- ½ t. garlic powder or minced garlic

1. Preheat oven to broil.
2. Season flounder with salt and pepper.
3. Melt butter in microwave.
4. Blend lemon juice and garlic into melted butter.
5. Baste flounder fillets with butter mixture.
6. Place fish on broiler pan and broil until fish is flaky (approximately 5 minutes).

Serves 4-5

I love meat
because
it's hearty...
I'm an
Oklahoma girl
who was raised
on meat
and potatoes!
— DENISE

CROCKPOT ROAST TENDERLOIN

from DENISE

This is a recipe that Heather Payne told me about when I was hosting my entire family for Christmas and needed some meal options. It tasted great and was not hard to do. It also made great leftovers for sandwiches!

- 1½ lb. pork tenderloin or pork roast
- 14½ oz. can beef broth
- 1/3 cup Worcestershire sauce
- 1/3 cup Frank's Red Hot Sauce

Sauce:
- ½ cup ketchup
- ½ cup molasses
- ¼ cup mustard
- ¼ cup Worcestershire sauce
- 2 T. Frank's Red Hot Sauce

1. Place roast in Crockpot and add the next 3 ingredients on top.
2. Cook on high for 5 hours.
3. Combine ingredients for sauce.
4. Heat in saucepan and serve over pork.

Serves 4-6

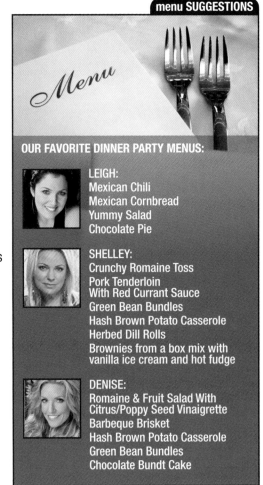

menu SUGGESTIONS

OUR FAVORITE DINNER PARTY MENUS:

LEIGH:
Mexican Chili
Mexican Cornbread
Yummy Salad
Chocolate Pie

SHELLEY:
Crunchy Romaine Toss
Pork Tenderloin
With Red Currant Sauce
Green Bean Bundles
Hash Brown Potato Casserole
Herbed Dill Rolls
Brownies from a box mix with vanilla ice cream and hot fudge

DENISE:
Romaine & Fruit Salad With Citrus/Poppy Seed Vinaigrette
Barbeque Brisket
Hash Brown Potato Casserole
Green Bean Bundles
Chocolate Bundt Cake

RARA'S POT ROAST

from LEIGH

Family traits aren't just in the way we look. They also show up in the "culinary gene pool." In my family, recipes have been passed down from generation to generation! This recipe has been conquered by many of us, but Rara's (that is what the grandkids call her, but she is Mom to me) is the best. Hers is the most tender and juiciest roast ever! (I will say my daddy and Aunt Billie Jo run a really close second.) Oftentimes, the roast would be accompanied by macaroni pie, lima beans, rice and gravy and fruit salad. I can see it sitting on the counter now, buffet style. Dig in! And if GREAT could get GREATER, it has. Mom now adds celery and a touch of garlic. Practice makes perfect they always say!!

- 2 T. vegetable oil
- 1½ lb. roast
- salt & pepper to taste
- 1 yellow onion, chopped
- 3 large carrots, sliced
- 4 medium potatoes, quartered

1. Preheat oven to 350.
2. Heat oil in large roasting pan or Dutch oven.
3. Sear roast on all sides.
4. After searing add chopped yellow onion.
5. Add enough water but not completely covering the roast (about 4 cups).
6. Bake for 2 hours, covered.
7. Add carrots and potatoes and cook for another hour – or until vegetables are tender. (If you want to spice it up even more - add some garlic in with the onion.) (Also, if you prefer cooking in the crockpot versus the oven do so after you sear the roast. You can leave it in the crockpot as long as you wish - just be sure to keep a healthy portion of water added in order to keep roast tender).

Rara has trained up her girls in the way they "should" cook... I'm still in training.

How can something so easy be soo fantastic?
You don't need an answer, just an appetite!

Serves 6

MARMALADE SLOW COOKER CHICKEN

Fix this in the morning and it's ready when you return home from work. The smell will welcome you home!

from LEIGH

- 2 sweet potatoes, peeled and diced
- 2 acorn squash, dice meaty inside part after seeds and pulp have been scooped out
- 2 leeks, chopped
- 4 skinless chicken breasts
- Salt and pepper to taste

Sauce:
- ½ cup chicken broth
- 2 heaping T. of orange marmalade

1. Layer in slow cooker as listed.
2. Combine sauce ingredients and pour on top.
3. Cook at least 3 hrs. on high or 6 to 8 hrs. on low.

Serves 4

PORK TENDERLOIN WITH RED CURRANT SAUCE

from SHELLEY

I have this reputation, at least among my singing cohorts and friends, that I am some gourmet, "Martha Stewart" type of cook. This is really not true at all! There are certain food magazines I won't even purchase because I know for a fact I won't have the correct "tools" required to pull off the recipes. I'm not about to spend 20 or 30 extra bucks at Williams-Sonoma just to buy some pastry blender that I will use once a year - maybe. The fact is, I just want to "appear" to be a good cook and make food that sounds difficult and impressive. That's my method of operation. Don't tell anyone. That's sorta what this recipe is to me! I mean, "Marinated Pork Tenderloin with Red Currant Sauce!" Sounds hard, doesn't it? But it's not!! My mom gave me this recipe a few years back and it's a hit every time. Pair it with some "Green Bean Bundles" from the vegetable chapter and you, too, will have your friends calling you "Martha" in no time!

- 2 lbs. pork tenderloin (this is usually packaged as two smaller tenderloins together)
- ½ cup soy sauce
- ½ cup cooking sherry
- 2 cloves garlic, minced
- 1 t. ground ginger
- 1 t. ground thyme
- 1 T. dry mustard

1. Mix together soy sauce, sherry, garlic, ginger, thyme, and dry mustard.
2. Place in large plastic zip bag along with the tenderloins. Shake bag to coat meat well.
3. Refrigerate overnight. (or at least 6 hours)
4. Pork can be grilled at a low grill setting for approximately two hours.
5. Slice and drizzle with red currant sauce before serving.

shelley, Caroline, Mom and Grandma Ruth...four generations of great cooks and "cooks to be!"

(Oven roasting method: pork can be placed in a shallow roasting pan and baked at 325 degrees, uncovered, for 1½ hours.)

Red Currant Sauce:
- 10 oz. jar red currant jelly
- 2 T. cooking sherry
- 1 t. soy sauce

1. Heat jelly, sherry and soy sauce in a small saucepan on medium heat until jelly is liquefied and all ingredients are combined.
2. Keep warm on low heat and drizzle over pork before serving.

Serves 6-8

HAWAIIAN GRILLED PORK CHOPS

from SHELLEY

I have never been a very good "griller" by nature. I have to say, however, after some tips from my brother-in-law Kyle, my husband David does a pretty good job for us. He has a few tricks and secrets for moist pork and chicken every time and his steaks just keep getting better. This recipe for the grill is no exception. It's a great main dish for company in the summer, or if you can talk someone into heating up the grill in the winter, this recipe will always please! I love to serve it with teriyaki rice and our Asian Cabbage Salad. (I just buy any old rice mix at the grocery store!) Fresh pineapple really makes it special, too, but I have used canned slices just as much!

- 1 (20 oz.) can pineapple slices, un-drained
- Six 1-inch thick pork chops
- ½ cup soy sauce
- ⅓ cup vegetable oil
- ¼ cup minced onion
- 1 clove garlic, minced
- 1 T. brown sugar

1. Drain pineapple reserving ¼ cup of juice. Set pineapple aside.
2. Place chops in large shallow dish.
3. Combine reserved pineapple juice and remaining 5 ingredients, mixing well.
4. Pour over chops.
5. Cover and marinate in refrigerator 2 hours or more.
6. Remove chops, reserving marinade.
7. Grill over medium coals 45 minutes, turning frequently and basting with marinade.
8. Place a pineapple ring on each chop during last few minutes of cooking time.

Serves 6

a quick POINT

More Grilling Tips:

1. Carefully rubbing the grill down with olive oil on a paper towel right before you put on the meat (olive oil has the highest "burning point" of all oils) will keep the meat from sticking to the grill. It also helps you get better "grill marks".

2. Approximate cooking times:
   - Chicken 20-25 minutes
   - Medium piece of steak (rib-eye, NY strip, etc.) 14 minutes
   - Hamburger (thick) 18 minutes
   - Pork tenderloin 30-45 minutes

3. Five Minute Rule - turn meat every 5 minutes for best results.

EASY CROCKPOT CHICKEN

from DENISE

This recipe makes me laugh. My babysitter/"adopted daughter" Jessie LOVES this chicken. She thought I worked on it all day. Ha! Little does she know! My secret is that I make this meal when I'm out all day and Jessie has to pick up the kids and feed them dinner. You can serve with rice or pasta and veggies.

- 4 frozen chicken breasts
- 1 pkg. of dry Italian dressing mix
- 1 cup warm water or chicken broth

1. All you do is stick the frozen breasts in the Crockpot.
2. Pour the dressing mix and then the water/broth on top of the chicken and cook on low for up to 10 hours.

The chicken is always nice and tender!

Serves 4

Stu, Price, Spence Denise and Jessie

OPEN FACE HAM SANDWICHES

from SHELLEY

These are the GREATEST little ham sandwiches you will ever eat. I absolutely love the broiled tomatoes and the yummy spread on them. Again, another one of my mom's standbys for a casual, Saturday lunch or even a light dinner with a salad or soup. We go to the beach every summer with my whole family and I always make these at least once. It's not that they are hard to make at all, but for some reason I don't think about making them much. Hopefully, now that I've highlighted them in my own cookbook, I will think of them more often!

- 8 oz. cream cheese, softened
- ½ cup butter or margarine, softened
- ½ cup grated Parmesan cheese
- 1 t. paprika
- ½ t. garlic powder
- ½ t. oregano
- 4 English muffins, split
- 8 slices of cooked ham, or deli-sliced ham (I use Boar's Head most of the time)
- 8 slices of tomato

1. Preheat oven to broil.
2. Combine cream cheese and butter. Stir till smooth.
3. Stir in cheese, paprika, oregano, and garlic powder.
4. Spread ⅔ of mixture evenly over cut surfaces of English muffins.
5. Top each with ham and tomato slices.
6. Spoon remaining cheese on center of each tomato slice.
7. Place on baking sheet, broil till golden brown, 5-10 minutes.

Serves 8

a quick POINT

Try this conversation starter at your next dinner party or night out with friends. Starting with the host or hostess, go around the table and take turns sharing what you would eat if you knew it was your last meal. Don't think of it as morbid! Think of it more as an icebreaker for people who may not all know each other and a great way to learn something new about your lifelong friends!

HERE ARE OUR LAST SUPPER WISHES:

SHELLEY: Well, of course you know it's going to be Mexican, hello??? Probably the least healthy thing in the world, but here it goes. After all, I'm about to die, so who cares? // **Appetizer:** California Pizza Kitchen's Bruschetta // **Entrée:** Las Palmas Chicken Chimichangas with White Cheese Sauce....a little salsa on the side....they are fried to a heavenly crisp.... // **Side dish:** Las Palmas Refried Beans with a side of pico de gallo // **Dessert:** Fried Donuts from The Patterson House here in Nashville. (but only on Thursday night, that chef really knows how to fry 'em)

LEIGH: My last supper would begin with a few appetizers and include MANY side dishes! // **Appetizers:** Avocado egg rolls from Cheesecake Factory accompanied with fresh chips and salsa from Garcia's (a Mexican rest. in Franklin, TN). // **Salad:** My salad choice would be a spinach Waldorf from America's in Houston, TX // **Entrée:** The main entree would be my Mom's cubed steak with brown rice and gravy // **Side dishes:** Aunt Billie Jo's Mackie pie, Mom's black eyed peas, dressing and gravy (when it is your last meal you can never have enough gravy!), Mom's creamed corn and her lima beans. // **Dessert:** The dessert would be Mom's chocolate pie! And off to glory I would go!

DENISE:
Appetizer: For starters I would begin with fried macaroni and cheese balls from the Cheesecake Factory and then I would have the "beef stew" from Cracker Barrel. // **Entrée:** My main meal is a little redundant as far as meat is concerned, but I am definitely a meat and potatoes girl. For the main course I would love my mom's OK barbeque brisket // **Side dishes:** hash brown potato casserole and Shelley's green bean bundles. // **Dessert:** I think I would end with something that isn't necessarily considered dessert, but I love it - Strawberry Pretzel Salad.

LAMB KABOBS (over rice pilaf)

from LEIGH

"Baa" Humbug! I am quite the Scrooge when it comes to Lamb. I think it has something to do with the fact that my sister (who is 11 months older than me) always requested it for her birthday meal. She knew how much I HATED it. In our family, if you didn't eat what was on the table, too bad, so sad. My Mom wasn't the type to microwave a hot dog just because someone didn't like the entrée. Fortunately, the Lamb Kabobs were accompanied with a rice pilaf. Maybe this is where my love for carbs started!

In all seriousness, I enjoy em' now and "taste" what my sister loved so much about them. Happy Birthday to me!!

Lamb Kabobs:
- 1 leg of lamb, cut into cubes
- 16 oz. bottle zesty Italian salad dressing
- 1 small onion chopped fine
- 1 T. minced garlic
- Two 15 oz. cans fire roasted tomatoes
- ½ cup water
- ½ t. thyme
- ½ t. basil
- salt
- pepper
- pinch sugar

see the "stinker look" in her eye?... she was always up to something... love ya sis!

1. Marinate lamb in gallon zip-lock bag overnight in Italian salad dressing with chopped onion and garlic.
2. Place lamb kabobs on skewers saving marinade. (You can also add tomatoes, peppers and other vegetables to the skewers)
3. Place skewers of lamb on grill and cook until done.
4. While lamb is grilling, pour marinade in 5 quart Dutch oven over medium heat.
5. Add tomatoes, thyme, basil, salt, pepper and sugar.
6. Bring to a boil then simmer over low heat for 10 minutes.
7. Add water as needed to avoid scorching.
8. When lamb is done add to sauce and keep warm until ready to serve. Serve over rice pilaf.

Rice Pilaf:
- 2 T. butter
- ½ cup crushed egg noodles
- 4 cups instant rice
- 4 cups chicken broth

1. Melt butter in a saucepan.
2. Add crushed egg noodles and saute' over low heat until noodles are golden brown.
3. Add chicken broth and bring to a boil.
4. Add instant rice, stir, then cover.
5. Remove from heat and let sit for 5 minutes.
6. Fluff rice before serving.

Serves 6-8

CHAPTER SIX

SO, YOU'RE SUPPOSED TO BRING A
SIDE DISH

Don't you just hate it when you get asked to bring the side dish for the potluck dinner, supper club or family picnic? Well, we feel the same way. That's why we have come up with some recipes that will upstage the entrée and dessert at any get-together!

BILLY JO'S MACKIE PIE

from LEIGH

This macaroni and cheese dish is another family recipe and a kid pleaser, too. It brings the goodness of home back to me every time I make it. Aunt Billie Jo doesn't have a recipe. She just "eyes it up" and our tummies enjoy it! Hope you will too.

Aunt Billie Jo

- 1 lb. box angel hair pasta
- 1 stick butter, divided use
- 16 oz. package sharp cheddar cheese, divided use
- 1 large egg
- 5 cups milk
- salt
- pepper

1. Preheat oven to 350.
2. Make angel hair pasta as instructed then drain.
3. Spray a 9x13 glass dish with non-stick cooking spray.
4. Begin the layering process: Layer ½ the pasta in baking dish.
5. Sprinkle salt and pepper.
6. Add pats of butter (4 T. per layer).
7. Next add a layer of extra sharp cheddar cheese (8 oz. per layer).
8. Repeat same ingredients for the next layer.
9. In a separate bowl whisk together one egg with approx. 5 cups of milk.
10. Now it's time to "eye it up." Start pouring the milk/egg mix. You need this liquid to sit just under the top layer of noodles to keep it from boiling over during baking. In other words, don't fill it all the way to the top.
11. Bake for 40 minutes.

Serves 8-10

GUESS WHO'S COMING TO LEIGH'S?

IF I COULD HAVE A DINNER PARTY AND INVITE ANYONE I WANTED, LIVING OR DEAD, I'D PICK:

VALENTINO SAMMARCO - this was Dana's "Poppy," whom he held in highest esteem. I'd love to hug and talk to the one that made such a powerful impact in the life of such a little boy.

MY GRANDMOTHER, ARLENE IVESTER — my mom's mother. She passed away just after I turned 2 years old. Rumor has it that to know her was to love her. Apparently, she was full of God's compassion and kindness.

MY HUSBAND AND MY DAUGHTER - I would hate for them not to celebrate such an inspirational time with me!

SWISS VEGETABLE MEDLEY

from SHELLEY

This recipe was passed on to me from our illustrious cookbook "ghost" writer, Julie. We trade recipes all the time and when she told me her family fights over this dish at Thanksgiving and Christmas, I knew it must be special. It's sooooooo good, but better than that, it's different. Not your same ol' mashed potatoes or green bean casserole. If Julie's family loves it and my family loves it, trust me, it's been through some tough taste testers! I'm confident you will love it too.

- 16 oz. bag frozen veggie mix with broccoli, carrots and cauliflower (thawed and drained)
- 1 can cream of mushroom soup
- 1 cup shredded Swiss cheese
- ½ cup sour cream
- 4 oz. jar pimentos
- 1 can (2.8 oz.) French fried onions

1. Preheat oven to 350.
2. Combine vegetables, soup, ½ the Swiss cheese, sour cream, pimentos and ½ the onions
3. Pour into 1 qt. baking dish.
4. Bake covered for 30 minutes
5. Uncover and top with remaining cheese and onions
6. Bake uncovered for 5-10 more minutes
   or until top is brown

Serves 6

VEGETABLE CASSEROLE WITH CREOLE SAUCE

from DENISE

My friend Karri had back surgery, which put her out of commission for almost 3 months. During that time, she was loved and taken care of by many sweet ladies who believe that a "holy" casserole is part of God's healing. This particular casserole was one of her very favorites. When I asked her about a side dish, she couldn't wait to share this recipe. She made it for Thanksgiving this year and she was right. It is amazing! I realize that looking at the ingredients you might think it's a little weird, but when it's all put together, it's a masterpiece.

Karri and Denise

Vegetable Casserole:
- 1 can baby lima beans, cooked with 1 T. butter, salt and pepper to taste
- 1 can small English peas, cooked with 1 T. butter, salt and pepper to taste
- 1 can French style green beans, cooked with 1 T. butter, salt and pepper to taste
- French fried onion rings, small can (2.8 oz.)

Sauce:
- 2 hard boiled eggs (grated)
- 1 t. mustard
- 1 t. Worcestershire sauce
- 1 cup mayonnaise
- 6 T. diced onions
- 4 T. vegetable oil
- dash of hot sauce

1. Preheat oven to 350.
2. In greased 9x13 casserole dish put layer of lima beans, sauce; layer of peas, sauce; layer of green beans, sauce.
3. Heat until bubbly (about 30 minutes).
4. Add can of French fried onions to top and brown (only 2-3 minutes).

Serves 8-10

GUESS WHO'S COMING TO DENISE'S?

IF I COULD HAVE A DINNER PARTY AND INVITE ANYONE I WANTED, LIVING OR DEAD, I'D PICK:

MY GRANDMOTHERS - They were wonderful, Godly women and taught me a lot. BUT, I wish that I could ask them questions about marriage and life that I didn't know to ask when they were alive.

MY COUSIN BRENT AND HIS WIFE MARCY - Brent has been my oldest and best friend. He makes me laugh harder than anyone else, except maybe Shelley. The bonus is that I love the girl he married, too. We don't get to see each other much anymore, so I would LOVE having them over for dinner.

ERIC TAYLOR (THE COACH FROM "FRIDAY NIGHT LIGHTS") - I love his character on the show and think he's totally cute! ☺

BUTTERNUT SQUASH CASSEROLE

from LEIGH

Every year, three of my girlfriends (Lori, Lisa and Rhonda) and I plan a vacation weekend. It doesn't matter where we go as long as we are together. A few years ago we planned our vacation in Nashville (at my house, actually). We had so much fun!! Instead of going out to eat one evening, we decided to go grocery shopping. Each one of us picked out something we wanted to fix. Lori decided to make butternut squash casserole. Fortunately, we all love butternut squash! What's not to love when you add all of these great ingredients together? It was so delicious and obviously quite memorable. I can't even remember what I fixed that night.

Casserole:
- 3 cups butternut squash (about 1 medium)
- ½ cup sugar
- ½ cup butter (1 stick)
- 2 eggs, beaten
- 1 teaspoon vanilla
- ⅓ cup milk

Topping:
- ¼ cup melted butter
- ¾ cup light brown sugar
- ½ cup flour
- ¾ cup chopped pecans

Lori, Rhonda, Lisa and Leigh about to feast on some serious Memphis BBQ ribs down the street. hmmmm hmmmm good!

1. Preheat oven to 350.
2. Cook butternut squash: Peel, cut in large chunks, & boil in water (barely covered) for 20-30 min. until soft. If you cook by boiling, it is very important to DRAIN WELL OR split squash in half lengthwise and remove seeds. Bake, cut side down, covered, in shallow baking dish with a small amount of water at 350 for 1 hour, or microwave on high 6 min. Allow to cool, then scoop out squash.
3. Mix together cooked squash, sugar, butter, eggs, vanilla, and milk.
4. Place in 13x9 baking dish.
5. Mix together ingredients for topping and sprinkle on top of squash mixture.
6. Bake for 35 minutes.

Serves 6

SPINACH & CHEDDAR SOUFFLÉ

from SHELLEY

I know you may think that you can't make a souffle'. It does sound hard, I will admit, but this souffle' is pretty foolproof and it is delicious! If you can separate a yolk from an egg white, you can make this dish (see this chapter's Cooking Class if you need help). It's sufficiently healthy, I mean with the spinach and all, but the cheese makes it more than bearable! Popeye would be proud!

- 10 oz. box frozen spinach, chopped, cooked and drained
- ¼ cup butter
- ¼ cup flour
- ½ t. salt
- ¾ cup milk
- 2 T. diced onions
- 4 eggs, separated
- 1 cup sharp cheddar cheese, grated

1. Preheat oven to 350.
2. Combine butter and flour over low heat, stir well until smooth and bubbly.
3. Add salt, pepper and milk and stir constantly over medium heat until smooth and thick.
4. Add cheese and stir until melted.
5. Remove from heat and add spinach and onion.
6. Gradually add egg yolks, let cool for 15 minutes.
7. Beat egg whites until stiff – about 3 or 4 minutes.
8. Fold egg whites into spinach mixture.
9. Pour into greased soufflé dish or other round, glass dish.
10. Bake for 35 minutes or until golden brown on top.

Serves 6-8

GUESS WHO'S COMING TO SHELLEY'S?

IF I COULD HAVE A DINNER PARTY AND INVITE ANYONE I WANTED, LIVING OR DEAD, I'D PICK:

BILLY GRAHAM - What an impact he has made on the world with his simple biblical wisdom. I would probably wear him out with my questions about his life!

BRITNEY SPEARS - I feel like we would be friends. I would love to just be a "normal" Godly friend to her.

HENRY HAKOLA (MY MOM'S DAD) AND JOE PHILLIPS (MY DAD'S DAD) - My two grandfathers who both died when I was very young. Now that I'm older I wish that I could pick their brain about my own father and mother.

MICHAEL JACKSON - I'd just like to go straight to the source and find out what really happened, not only in his death, but his mysterious life. He seems like he would be a nice enough guy.

DAYNA'S SOUR CREAM & SQUASH CASSEROLE

from DENISE

When I was growing up you couldn't have paid me to eat anything with squash in it. So, I can't get on to my own kids for not eating it. Well, taste buds do change because I LOVE it now. When my friends who have gardens have too much squash, I beg for some of the extras so that I can make this casserole.

- 4 cups yellow squash, chopped
- 1 cup onion, chopped
- 1 can cream of mushroom soup
- ½ cup margarine, melted
- 1 cup sour cream
- 8 oz. pkg. of stuffing mix

1. Preheat oven to 350 degrees.
2. Cook squash in a small amount of water in a saucepan until tender.
3. Drain.
4. Stir in soup, sour cream and onion.
5. Combine margarine and stuffing mix in another bowl, toss to mix.
6. Cover bottom of greased baking dish with half the stuffing mixture.
7. Spoon in squash mix.
8. Top with remaining stuffing mixture.
9. Bake for 35 minutes.

Serves 10-12

Dayna and Denise

CORNBREAD CASSEROLE

from DENISE

Some days you get bored with the same potato casserole or rice dish. You want to serve a starch with your meal, but don't know what. Well, here is the solution: Cornbread Casserole. It's a delicious combination of cornbread and corn casserole all mixed in one heavenly dish.

- 8 oz. cream cheese
- 1 stick butter
- medium onion, diced
- ½ red bell pepper, diced thin
- 1 can whole kernel corn
- 1 can cream style corn
- 3 eggs
- 1 box corn muffin mix
- 1/8 t. black pepper

1. Preheat oven to 350.
2. Soften (don't melt) cream cheese and butter together in microwave for about 1½ minutes in large bowl.
3. Remove from microwave and stir 'til mixed well
4. Add onion, peppers, corn, creamed corn, muffin mix and black pepper.
5. Add eggs and mix well.
6. Pour into 9x13 baking dish and bake for 45-50 minutes or until golden brown on top.

Serves 10

MOM'S THANKSGIVING DRESSING & GRAVY

from LEIGH

Cornmeal is a part of my family heritage. My Great Granddaddy Ivester owned a small cornmeal store back in the late 1800's. The store is no longer standing but I still have the cornmeal sack they used for the consumer. You can imagine all the delicious uses for cornmeal that my family perfected. One was the Thanksgiving dressing that always accompanied the turkey. This dressing was topped with a blanket of giblet gravy. Mmmm, mmmm GOOD!!! In all of my travels I have NEVER tasted anything like it. As a matter of fact, when I married a Yankee from New York I was shocked the first time I had stuffing instead of dressing for Thanksgiving! I had never heard of such a thing! I was so confused. (Of course I used my southern manners and kept my opinion to myself.) After 17 years of marriage I have acquired a taste for stuffing. It's not bad, but I still prefer my Mom's Thanksgiving Dressing And Gravy.

NOTE: Mom always stews a hen or chicken pieces with 2 stalks of celery and 1 whole onion when she makes dressing. This gives you the stock you need for the dressing and the giblet gravy.

- 8x8 pan of cornbread, crumbled
- 1½ cups crumbled white bread (loaf, biscuits, sandwich buns etc.)
- 1 T. sage
- 1 stick butter or margarine
- 1 medium onion, chopped fine
- 2 stalks celery and the onion from stewed chicken, chopped
- 1 cup chicken stock
- 2 cans chicken broth
- milk

1. Preheat oven to 350.
2. Melt butter and onion together in skillet.
3. Stir to coat onion and cook until onion is tender.
4. Mix crumbled breads and sage together.
5. Pour melted butter and onions into crumbled bread mixture.
6. Add stock from stewed chicken along with the chopped celery and onion.
7. Add chicken broth and mix.
8. Add milk as needed to make mixture very "wet".
9. Pour into 9x13 baking dish and bake until dressing is brown and set, approximately 30 to 45 minutes.

Giblet Gravy:
- 3 T. all purpose flour
- 1 cup water
- 1 boiled egg
- stewed chicken liver, chopped

1. Gradually mix water and flour to form a smooth paste.
2. Thin with remaining water. Whisk flour mixture into boiling chicken stock until desired consistency.
3. Add chopped egg and chopped liver.
4. Serve over dressing.

Serves 8-10

Soooooo goooooooooood!!!

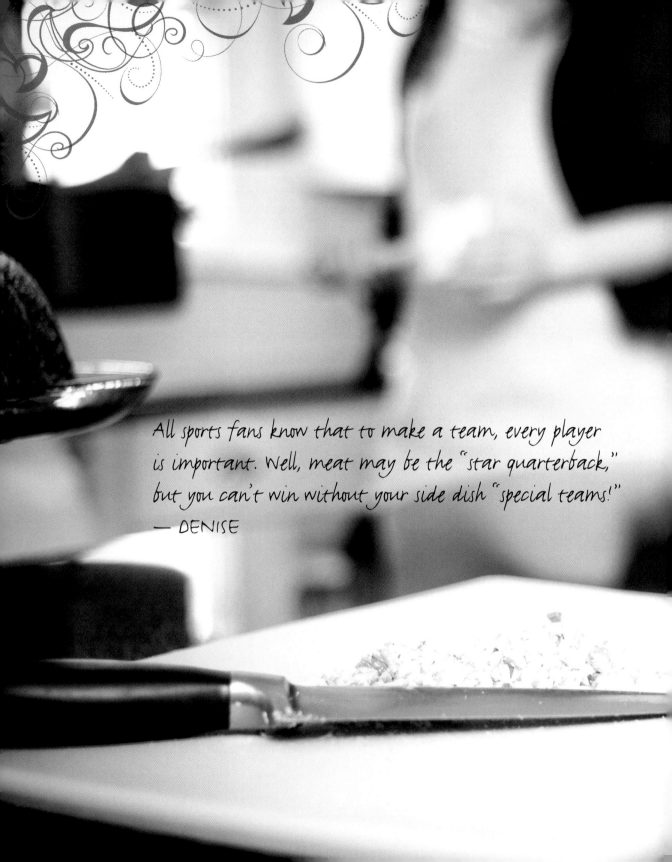

All sports fans know that to make a team, every player is important. Well, meat may be the "star quarterback," but you can't win without your side dish "special teams!"
— DENISE

QUICK HERBED DILL ROLLS

from SHELLEY

When we were putting together the recipes for this cookbook, we didn't really have enough bread recipes for a whole chapter devoted to bread. However, this recipe kept popping up for one reason or another. I have served these rolls to many of my friends on different occasions and we all just decided they were too good to not include! My mom gave me this recipe a few years back and it just puts a little extra impressive touch on what would normally be a part of the dinner you don't pay much attention to, the bread. These rolls are so easy and taste like buttery balls of herbed goodness! When I was giving Julie (our co-author extraordinaire!) the recipe just the other night for a dinner party she was attending, she could hardly believe that you just used canned biscuits to make these. She thought I made the dough myself with yeast and the whole nine yards. I told her she should know me better than that! I just want it to taste DELICIOUS, look DIFFICULT, and be EASY as pie! These rolls fit the bill!

- 11 oz. can refrigerated buttermilk biscuit dough
- ½ cup butter
- 1½ t. dried parsley flakes
- ½ t. dill weed (I add more than that because I love dill!)
- 1 T. onion flakes
- 2 T. parmesan cheese (from the can, not the fancy stuff)

1. Preheat oven to 425.
2. Melt butter in small saucepan.
3. Stir spices into it.
4. Remove from burner and let it set for 15-30 minutes.
5. Quarter each biscuit and arrange pieces in round cake pan. (It is okay if the biscuits are touching)
6. Pour mixture over the biscuits.
7. Bake for 10-12 minutes.

Serves 8-10

COOKING CLASS #6

"EGGS"CELLENT TIPS ABOUT COOKING WITH EGGS:

Temper, Temper! When you see a recipe that calls for "eggs, beaten and tempered", don't worry, this is not meant to be violent! When you are adding eggs to a hot mixture, such as squash casserole, if you add the egg straight into the mixture it will scramble! Unless you don't mind scrambled eggs in your casserole, you will need to do the following:
1. Crack the egg into a small bowl and beat with a fork or whisk.
2. Scoop about 1 cup of the hot mixture into the small bowl of beaten egg.
3. Mix well, then pour egg mixture into the hot mixture and mix well.

Don't make me separate you! When you are instructed to "separate the eggs", it is not because the eggs have been naughty and can't get along! It is because the egg and the yolk can serve two separate purposes. Eggs are really quite miraculous that way! The yolk acts to make the ingredients "hold together" and the whites, once beaten and folded in, act to make the dish fluffy. Here is how you separate an egg:
1. Crack the egg over a bowl, then hold halves of shell in each hand, being careful not to spill the contents (or at least not very much of it!).
2. Very carefully transfer the yolk (yellow part) from one shell to the other allowing egg whites to fall into the bowl below during the process.
3. When you are left with only yolk, place it in a separate bowl.

Mt. Egg White: After you have separated the eggs you will probably be asked to beat the egg whites until "stiff" or until they form "peaks". All this means is that you will need to beat those egg whites with a hand mixer for a good amount of time. They will take on a thick, fluffy texture. The test to see if they are ready is this: dip a spoon down to the bottom of the bowl and scoop upwards out of bowl. If egg whites form a little white mountain peak, your mission is accomplished!

BROCCOLI & CHEESE CASSEROLE

from DENISE

I would never eat broccoli growing up. I thought it was the grossest food in the world. However, when I was having a baby there was a ministry at my church that delivered frozen meals for those who had babies. Someone brought us this and I quickly changed my mind about broccoli! (A big hint: When you bring someone a meal, always include the recipe. It's so nice to be able to have the recipe when you taste something that you really like!)

- 20 oz. frozen, chopped broccoli
- 1 can cream of mushroom soup
- 3 T. minced onion
- 2 eggs, beaten
- 1 cup mayonnaise
- 1 cup sharp cheddar cheese, grated
- 1 stick butter, melted
- 1 sleeve buttery crackers, crushed

1. Preheat oven to 350.
2. Cook broccoli according to package, cool and drain.
3. Combine remaining ingredients except butter and crackers.
4. Pour into a greased 1-quart casserole dish and top with crackers that have been tossed with butter.
5. Bake for 30 minutes uncovered.

Serves 6

TOMATO PIE

from SHELLEY

Whenever I tell someone I am making a Tomato Pie, they usually look at me really funny and act like I'm crazy or something. I realize it may sound a little weird, but this is an absolutely delectable side dish that will wow your friends with its deliciousness!! It's so easy and is especially good when tomatoes are at their peak in the summertime.

It calls for one of my favorite herbs, basil. Buying fresh basil can be a little pricey but I have had great luck with growing my own. I usually start with a little $3 plant from the grocery store. All you have to do is pot it, water it, give it some sun and watch it grow. It's seriously super easy, as basil is a relatively hearty little plant. I love having it right outside my back door whenever I need it. Trust me, I am not bragging or trying to sound like Martha Stewart, nor am I trying to give the impression that I also "garden." That's a big fat joke. Basil and mint, that's about it for me. Any other plants are dead on arrival, for sure. It's always time to lament the end of summer when my basil plants start to die.

Anyway, I have served this pie alongside chicken salad and fruit at many daytime get-togethers. Just make sure you give it a good ten minutes or so after removing it from the oven. This will help it "settle" and be a little less juicy.

- 4 tomatoes, sliced
- 10 or more chopped fresh basil leaves
- 3 chopped green onions
- 9 inch frozen, deep dish pie shell
- kosher salt and freshly ground pepper
- 1 cup grated mozzarella cheese
- 1 cup grated cheddar cheese
- 1 cup of mayonnaise (Leigh told me about Duke's one time, and I have NEVER bought another brand since. It's SOOOO good.)

1. Preheat oven to 350.
2. Bake pie crust for 10-15 min. or until just starting to brown.
3. Layer the sliced tomatoes, basil and green onion in the pie shell.
4. Sprinkle with salt and pepper to taste.
5. Combine cheeses and mayonnaise.
6. Spread on top of tomatoes. (Almost like a frosting!)
7. Bake pie for 30 minutes or until the pie is lightly browned and bubbly.
8. Let set for 10 minutes before slicing.

Serves 8

PINEAPPLE SOUFFLÉ

from LEIGH

Being from a really small town, my family is always trying to come up with something fun to do. My sister Dana (remember, we have lots of Dana's in our lives) talked us into doing "theme dinners." We did our first one in her home with just a few family members. Now we do them at her church in Belton, SC, with over 50 peeps. It is becoming quite the family tradition. This year we did "Panic at the Prom." The dinner theme was a Luau so all the guests dressed up in their Luau attire ready for food, fellowship and so much fun! Staying as close as we could to "Hawaiian" style food my sister Reide made this delicious pineapple casserole. It is my favorite food combination: sweet and salty. Give it a try with any entree or have a theme dinner yourself. Have the whole family dress Hawaiian-style. The kids will love it!

- 2 cans pineapple chunks
- 5 T. flour
- ½ cup sugar
- 1 stick of butter
- 1½ cup sharp cheddar cheese, grated
- 1½ cup crushed buttery crackers

1. Preheat oven to 350.
2. Drain pineapple and pour into a casserole dish sprayed with cooking spray.
3. Heat pineapple juice, flour, and sugar in microwave until thickened.
4. Pour over pineapple.
5. Sprinkle cheese on top.
6. Put crackers on top of cheese.
7. Pour melted butter over crackers.
8. Bake for 30 minutes.

Serves 6-8

Prom King and Queen, Mark and Reide Buffington, Leigh's sister and brother-in-law

GREEN BEAN BUNDLES

from SHELLEY

These little bundles of joy (and I'm not talking about babies here) have become quite iconic for Breen dinner parties. Pretty much anything wrapped in bacon is good to me. Yes, these technically are a "vegetable". There are green beans in there somewhere, but let's be honest; they are basically just something to wrap the bacon around and soak in brown sugar and butter for 45 minutes. They do look impressive and my little hint would be to buy the Del Monte brand of whole green beans. They seem to be the longest ones in a can and make this dish a little easier to prepare.

My mom passed this recipe down to my sister Robyn and me. We both make them all the time for family gatherings or when we are entertaining our own friends. She and I are so lucky to have a mom who is an endless resource for good recipes! These beans are a staple at our family gatherings as well. I was so happy to have my whole family spend Christmas in Nashville with us in 2009. It was the first time ever and we made such wonderful memories. I will treasure that particular Christmas in my heart forever. Robyn and I kept the "Bundle Tradition" alive in my kitchen on Christmas day and as usual, there was not a single one left! Even the kiddos love this one! If anyone ever figures out a calorie count on one bundle, let me know. I think it would be shockingly funny! On second thought, never mind...

- 3 cans Del Monte whole green beans, drained (you can use a different brand, but don't say I didn't warn you!)
- ½ pound bacon
- ¾ stick of butter
- ½ C. brown sugar
- ½ t. salt
- ½ t. pepper
- 1 t. garlic powder

1. Preheat oven to 350.
2. Pour green beans in large bowl.
3. Cut bacon strips into thirds.
4. "Bundle" 5 or 6 beans together and wrap bacon around them.
5. Place in 9x13 baking dish.
6. Repeat this assembly process until dish is full (some beans will be too small for bundles and these will be left over).
7. In small saucepan melt butter.
8. Add brown sugar, salt, pepper and garlic powder and simmer for 5 minutes.
9. Pour mixture over green bean bundles.
10. Bake for 45 minutes.

Serves 8-10

Shelley, Robyn and the beloved bundles

LUCY'S SWEET & SOUR GREEN BEANS

from DENISE

Sometimes it's really hard to find a new way to cook green beans. Well, that's what friends are for. My friend Lucy gave me a great recipe to change up the monotony of the same old side dish. She made Sweet & Sour Green Beans for a dinner party and I fell in love with them. These ingredients give plain green beans a little kick. Depending on what kind of mood you are in that day, you can play around with the ingredients by adding a little more sugar for sweetness or you can add more vinegar for a little more punch.

- 6 cans green beans, drained
- ½ cup cider vinegar
- ¾ cup sugar
- ½ lb. bacon
- 1 large onion cut into thin rings

1. Fry bacon.
2. Remove from pan and take grease off heat.
3. Mix vinegar and sugar. Add to grease.
4. Transfer to a large pot. Place onions in grease mixture and saute until limp.
5. Add beans and stir.
6. Cook 30 minutes or more stirring frequently.

They are best if made a day ahead and refrigerated. The beans soak up more flavor. Just reheat and eat!

Serves 8-10

Denise and Lucy

HASH BROWN CASSEROLE

from DENISE

This is my husband's favorite thing to eat. Sometimes it's the only way to get him to go to a party that he isn't excited about attending. It goes great with almost any kind of meal and everyone loves it! I first tasted hash brown casserole when I was in college. I was in a singing group called the "Ouachitones." The director of the group was Mrs. Mary Shambarger. She was a wonderful, classy woman and a fabulous cook. Every year for Christmas, she would invite all of the girls in the group over for a delicious meal. Hash brown casserole was always a hit!

Casserole:
- 32 oz. package of hash brown potatoes, thawed (I usually get the shredded kind)
- 2 cups shredded cheddar cheese
- ½ cup chopped onion
- 1 can cream of chicken soup
- 16 oz. sour cream
- ¼ cup butter, melted
- salt and pepper to taste

Topping:
- 2 cups of crushed corn flakes
- 3 T. butter, melted
- paprika

1. Preheat oven to 350.
2. Mix hash browns with all ingredients and place in greased 9x13 casserole dish.
3. Mix cornflakes and melted butter and place on top of hash brown mixture.
4. Sprinkle a little paprika over the top.
5. Bake 45 minutes lightly covered with foil.
6. Take foil off and bake another 15 minutes.

Serves 8-10

a quick POINT

THE BALANCED PLATE: Always try to serve something green with every dinner. This creates a balanced plate when it comes to presentation as well as health considerations!

A good rule of thumb is to serve one starchy side dish, such as potatoes, pasta or rice and one non-starchy side, such as a salad, vegetable casserole or green beans.

SWEET POTATO CASSEROLE

from LEIGH

This casserole is so deliciously sweet that it almost belongs in the dessert chapter! However, it is best when served with your favorite meat. It is very versatile and not only works great with turkey, but also with chicken, steak, pork and fish. Also, there are pecans in the topping and you know how I love my pecans!

- 6 or 7 small sweet potatoes (you want to end up with 3 cups cooked)
- 1 cup sugar
- 2 eggs, beaten and tempered (see Cooking Class in this chapter)
- ½ stick butter
- ½ cup milk
- 1 T. vanilla
- ½ t. salt

Topping:
- ½ cup brown sugar
- ½ cup flour
- ½ stick butter, softened
- 1 cup pecans, chopped

1. Preheat oven to 350.
2. Peel and slice sweet potatoes and place in medium pot.
3. Cover with water and boil until tender.
4. Drain sweet potatoes, add butter and mash.
5. Add sugar, eggs, milk, vanilla and salt. Mix well.
6. Pour into greased, 2-quart baking dish.
7. Mix sugar and flour. Cut in butter until crumbly. (See Cooking Class in Dessert Chapter)
8. Stir in pecans and sprinkle over sweet potatoes.
9. Bake for 35 minutes.

Serves 6-8

CARROT SOUFFLÉ

from SHELLEY

I remember a few years back I REALLY wanted a food processor for my birthday. I just loved the big ol' mack daddy kind you see the cooks using on the Food Network. I would read recipes in my gourmet cooking magazine, which I loved, but I could never make half of them because I didn't have a food processor. Well, the girls went in together with Cheri, our manager at the time, and bought me one! I couldn't wait to use it and this is the first recipe I ever tried with it. It turned out delicious and I have made it several times since. It's light and fluffy and tastes sweet, almost like sweet potatoes. You could even make it in place of sweet potatoes for Thanksgiving and no one would bat an eye. Also, you will need two soufflé dishes because it makes a ton. I have never tried to half it and when you taste it, you'll see why. I promise, you will want it all!

3 lbs. carrots, peeled and sliced
2 cups sugar
3 sticks butter
6 large eggs
1⁄2 cup flour
3 t. baking powder
1⁄4 t. ground cinnamon

1. Preheat oven to 350.
2. Lightly grease two 1½-quart baking dishes.
3. Boil carrots until tender, then drain.
4. Combine all ingredients in food processor and pulse until smooth.
5. Spread mixture into baking dishes.
6. Bake for 1 hour or until set.
7. Serve immediately.

Serves 10-12

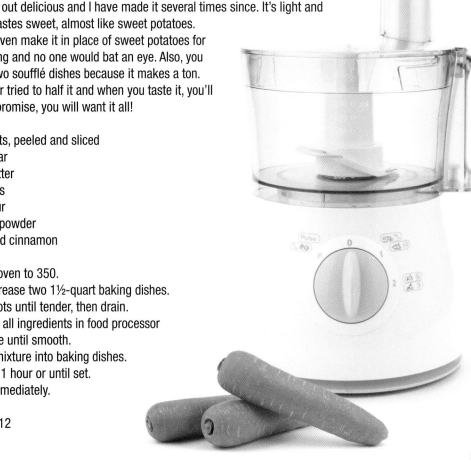

GRANDMA CANDY'S COWBOY BEANS

from SHELLEY

I just love potlucks and big family gatherings. My husband is from Michigan and though we don't get up there as much as we wish we could, I always love making the trip. I am fortunate to have TWO awesome mothers-in-law who live there and they are both great cooks! Last year, for Caroline's birthday, one set of in-laws came down to Nashville to help celebrate. We rented huge blow up water slides and bouncy houses for the kids and it was an all day family affair.

I had everyone bring a dish to pass, so Grandma Candy offered to make up a batch of Cowboy Beans. They sounded great, so I said "sure," but I had no idea just how good they would be. I had actually made several dishes that day, but all I heard my friends talk about were beans, beans, beans! They are hearty enough for a meal by themselves and sweet enough to be a dessert, to boot! (No pun intended!) So, if you want to be the hit of the family picnic or potluck, just make up a dish of these bad boys. Let me warn you, it makes a FULL 9x13 pan, and then some. (Probably another 8x8 to be exact.) But go ahead and make the whole recipe and bless somebody with the other pan!

- 2 lbs. ground beef
- 2 onions, sliced thinly
- 1 green pepper, chopped
- seasoned salt (such as Lawry's)
- 1 t. garlic powder
- 2 family sized cans of pork and beans, at least 22 ounces each
- 2 T. mustard
- 2 cups brown sugar (1½ cups is fine for a little less sweetness)
- 36 oz. bottle of ketchup
- 1 lb. thinly sliced polish sausage

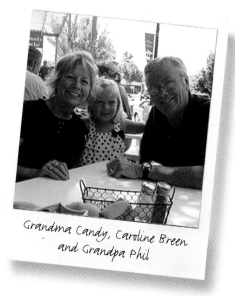

Grandma Candy, Caroline Breen and Grandpa Phil

1. Preheat oven to 350.
2. Brown ground beef, onions and green pepper.
3. Drain off grease.
4. Add garlic powder and season to taste with salt, pepper and seasoning salt.
5. In large bowl, add meat mixture to remaining ingredients. Mix well.
6. Spoon into 9x13 pan (plus 8x8 pan if there is extra) and bake uncovered for 1½ hours.

Serves 18-20

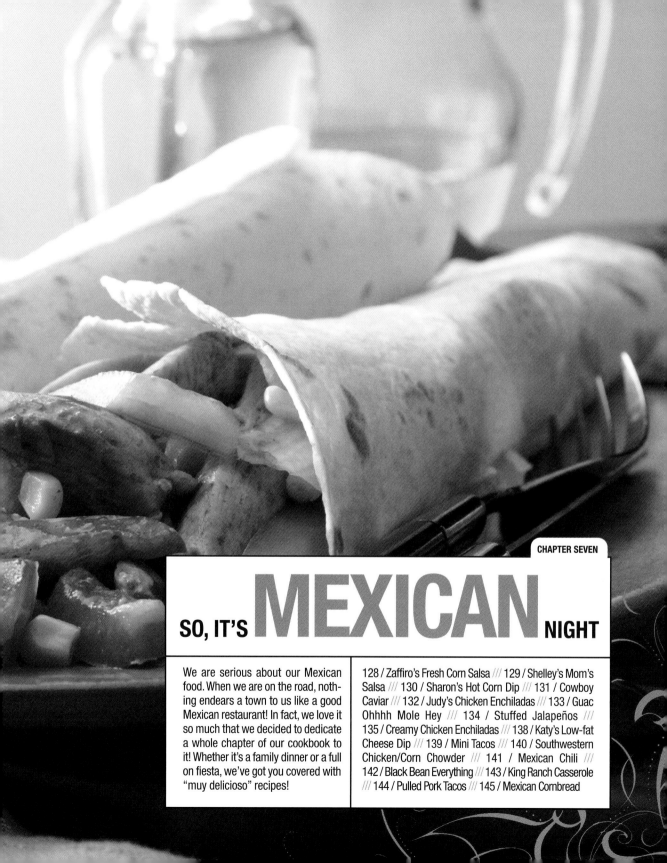

CHAPTER SEVEN

SO, IT'S MEXICAN NIGHT

We are serious about our Mexican food. When we are on the road, nothing endears a town to us like a good Mexican restaurant! In fact, we love it so much that we decided to dedicate a whole chapter of our cookbook to it! Whether it's a family dinner or a full on fiesta, we've got you covered with "muy delicioso" recipes!

ZAFFIRO'S FRESH CORN SALSA

from LEIGH

David Zaffiro is a very talented musician and producer but his wife Susan is the talent in the kitchen. Point Of Grace worked with David on our "I Choose You" record a few years ago. David was our producer and it is very common for a producer to have a home studio. This allows them to be home more with flexible hours, not to mention allowing the artists to raid the fridge. And did we EVER!!! Susan had a weekly menu. Wednesday was Taco/Mexican night. If we were still recording around suppertime, we were invited to join in the "eats." (You can imagine how many times we made sure we were NOT done before suppertime rolled around.) Susan had many memorable dishes but this one in particular was a POG favorite. Her corn salsa was out of this world. The leftovers were devoured the next day after each vocal session. Whoever didn't have to sing at the time was chowin' down with some chips. You have to try this. It is sooo fantastic and it's helps you sing better too. The fresh cilantro opens up the nasal passages! Ahhhhhh ahhhhhhhh!! Can't you hear it? Sounds like an angel.

(I usually double this recipe. Trust me, it's so good it just doesn't make enough!)

- 3 ears of fresh corn
- ½ onion, chopped
- one bunch cilantro, chopped
- 1 tomato, chopped
- juice of one lime
- 1 t. sugar
- dash of salt to taste

1. Cook the corn and cool.
2. Cut off of cob and place in bowl.
3. Add remaining ingredients and refrigerate for at least an hour so flavors can meld together.
4. Serve with chips.

Also delicious on top of fish or chicken!

Serves 6

David and Susan Zaffiro

SHELLEY'S MOM'S SALSA

from SHELLEY

Everyone knows how much Point of Grace likes Mexican food. I wasn't a huge fan until college and I'm pretty sure my love affair with all things Mex began with this recipe. It has made its way all around Nashville and is commonly known as "Shelley's Mom's Salsa." My friends all swear my mother sneaks an addictive substance into it because it's very hard to stop eating it once you start. My mom always makes a big batch of it before our Christmas tour and takes one over to the crew bus. I hear it usually only lasts a couple of nights on the guys' bus. Well, that's nothing! We down ours before the bus ever leaves Nashville! It has a restaurant salsa quality, but even better.

One Christmas the girls and I had the bright idea to make this salsa and can it as Christmas gifts for everyone at our record label. We each made several batches, canned it, bought a bunch of chips and delivered at least 50 jars of the stuff up to Word Records. In hindsight, it would have been much easier to just send a fruit basket, but not nearly as good. And hey, that's just the kind of people we are!

- Four 28 oz. cans Hunts Whole Tomatoes (Use Hunt's, other brands just don't taste the same)
- 3 T. + 1 t. vinegar
- 2 T. + 1 t. salt
- 5 T. of chopped jalapeno peppers
- 1 small onion, chopped
- 1 t. cumin powder
- 1 t. coriander powder
- 1 medium clove garlic, crushed

1. Puree tomatoes in blender, one can at a time, for only 3-4 seconds each. Do not puree any longer or salsa will be too runny.
2. Pour into large pan.
3. Add remaining ingredients and simmer on the stove for 15-30 minutes.
4. Store in refrigerator for up to 10 days. You may want to share some with your friends and neighbors because it makes a ton!

Serves 20 + people

shelley and her mom, sharon

SHARON'S HOT CORN DIP

from SHELLEY

I just LOVE anything that is hot and cheesy! Anything! My mom made this on Christmas Eve one year when we were in Little Rock. You need to serve it warm right out of the oven. No need to keep it over a warmer, it won't last that long!

- 2 cans of mexi-corn, drained
- 1 large jar of pimentos
- 1 bunch green onions, chopped
- ¼ cup diced jalapeno peppers
- 1½ cups sour cream
- 1 cup mayonnaise
- 1 t. garlic powder
- 1 t. Accent (can be found on spice aisle)
- 1 pound shredded cheddar cheese

1. Preheat oven to 350.
2. Mix together all ingredients.
3. Pour into a greased 9x13 pan.
4. Bake for 15 minutes.
5. Stir and bake for another 15 minutes.
6. Serve warm with corn chips.

Serves 8-10

COOKINGCLASS #7

MAKING YOUR OWN TORTILLA CHIPS: Make your next Mexican Night extra special by serving homemade chips with the guacamole and salsa. The end result is quite impressive, but they are actually easy to make!

You will need:
- 10 corn or flour tortillas (or both!)
- 3 T. vegetable oil
- small skillet
- Sea salt

1. Heat the vegetable oil in a small skillet over medium high heat. You know the oil is heated if it sizzles and pops when you flick a few drops of water into it.
2. Take a tortilla and put it in the skillet and turn heat down to medium.
3. The tortilla will start to "bubble" after about 15 seconds.
4. Flip the tortilla using tongs. Cook for another 15 seconds and flip again. (It may take several flips until tortilla looks golden brown and crunchy.)
5. Place cooked tortilla on chopping board and cut into 4-6 triangles with pizza cutter, like you would cut a pizza. (Go ahead and toss another tortilla into the pan while you are cutting the cooked tortilla.)
6. Blot some of the oil off of chips with a paper towel.
7. Put chips on a plate covered with a paper towel.
8. Repeat this process until you have cooked all the tortillas. (You may need to drizzle more oil into the skillet about halfway through the process.)
9. Sprinkle sea salt lightly on chips.
10. You can keep the chips warm in an oven set on low. If you would like to "crisp up" your chips some more, put them on a cookie sheet and bake at 300 for about 5 minutes. Let sit for 5 minutes. (They will get crispier as they sit out.)

COWBOY CAVIAR

from LEIGH

Mamas, DO let your babies grow up to eat Cowboy Caviar. Too good and too easy! After living in Nashville for over 15 years, anything that looks country or sounds country is definitely worth trying. The irony here is that I got this very Mexican recipe from Dana's godmother, Aunt Donna, who happens to be a New York Italian! YEEE HAW!!!!!

- 2 avocados, cut into cubes
- 1 tomato diced
- 11 oz. can shoe peg corn or petite white corn, drained
- 15 oz. can black-eyed peas, drained and rinsed
- ⅔ cup fresh cilantro - leaves only, chopped
- 3 green onions, chopped

1. Combine above in a bowl.

Dressing:
- ¼ cup olive oil
- ¼ cup red wine vinegar
- 2 cloves garlic, minced
- ½ t. cumin
- splash of lemon juice
- ¾ t. salt
- ⅛ t. black pepper
- 1 t. Worcestershire sauce
- Hot sauce to taste

2. Combine all in separate container.
3. Add to avocado mixture.
4. Stir and chill for at least two hours.
5. Serve with your favorite tortilla chips.

Serves 6-8

Aunt Donna with Dana

Aunt Donna and Uncle Bill with POG

JUDY'S CHICKEN ENCHILADAS

from DENISE

Growing up, I spent a lot of time at time at Mrs. Judy's house because her daughter Laura was one of my best friends. Judy was an amazing cook and she always made me try things that were outside of my comfort zone. I can remember sitting around their dinner table eating these enchiladas and having to sit on a phone book because I wasn't quite tall enough. The family referred to me most often as "Mini Masters" (my maiden name). Laura fought an amazing battle with diabetes.

She inspired people and brought laughter and smiles no matter how bad she felt. Although she may have lost her physical eyesight, her vision for God's purpose in her life was crystal clear. I am a better person because of her. She now resides with Jesus complete and whole, and I look forward to the day we will see each other again.

- 2 cups cooked chicken (chopped)
- 2 cups taco sauce
- 1 small can green chiles
- 1 pint half and half
- 1 T. chicken bouillon granules
- 8 oz. Monterey Jack cheese (shredded)
- 10-12 flour tortillas

1. Preheat oven to 350.
2. Mix taco sauce, green chiles and chicken together.
3. Heat half & half in saucepan to dissolve bouillon.
4. Dip tortilla in half and half.
5. Place a spoonful of chicken mixture in a tortilla. Roll up tight.
6. Place in baking dish.
7. After all the tortillas are placed, pour the rest of the half and half over the tortillas.
8. Sprinkle the cheese on top.
9. Bake 30 min.

Serves 8-10

Laura and Denise

Laura, Judy, Dayna and Denise

GUAC OHHHH MOLE HEY

from SHELLEY

Even though I travel a lot for a living, I still love to travel for pleasure! Not long ago, my husband had some business to do in New York City, so I quickly volunteered to go along with him. We decided to make a weekend out of it: a little shopping, a lot of eating! Just the way I like it! As you can imagine, the choice for fine dining establishments is endless in New York City, but sometimes, old habits die hard. Our first night there, with literally an entire world of eating options before us, we sought out a little Mexican restaurant in Soho on the recommendation of our friends, Rann and Kristen. Imagine the grief I got when I twittered "Having fun in New York! Eating great guac at Dos Cominos." My "foodie" friends were appalled that we were eating at a Mexican joint when every five star restaurant in the world was within walking distance!! But you know what? We didn't care.

That's nothing in comparison to our final night of a European vacation with our friends Jeff and Gayla several years ago. We opted out of a trip in Milan to see the world famous "Last Supper" painting. Instead, we took a cab ride 30 miles outside of town to a Mexican restaurant! I know that's really bad, but I was da Vinci'd out at that point. You can only see so many famous paintings 'til your eyes start crossing and you just want a taco.

Anyway, back to NYC! They actually give out the recipe at Dos Cominos for their world famous, tableside guacamole. My friend Keely has taken the recipe, tweaked it just a bit and turned it into what really is the world's best guacamole. Trust me, I eat Mexican food in Italy!

- 1 bunch of fresh cilantro
- 1 lime
- ½ t. kosher salt, coarse
- ½ purple onion, finely diced
- 2 cloves of garlic, finely diced
- 2 plum tomatoes, roughly chopped and seeded
- 1 serano chile pepper, finely diced, seeds removed
- 1 jalapeño pepper, finely diced, seeds removed
- 7 avocados, ripe

1. Press cilantro, garlic, onions, peppers, ½ t. salt and the juice of ½ the lime in a bowl with the back of a spoon.
2. Add tomatoes and stir.
3. Add avocados and mash together until smooth. (I like to use an avocado masher - it is oh so handy! If you don't have one, you can use a fork or a potato masher.)
4. Add additional cilantro, salt, pepper and limejuice to taste.

Tip: To keep your Guac fresh through the night and into the next day, take the pit of one of the avocados and bury it in the guacamole. It's a nice little Texas trick from Keely!

Serves 8-10

STUFFED JALAPEÑOS

from SHELLEY

These make a great and impressive appetizer for any party! CAUTION!! Do not clean and prepare peppers without latex gloves!!! TRUST ME ON THIS! I spent the entire night with my hands in bowls of ice water the first time I made these. I seriously wanted to check myself into the Vanderbilt Hospital Burn Unit. Don't try to be a hero! Wear gloves! I will say, however, they are so good, they were almost worth the torture. But if you can cook something without torture involved, I say "why not?"

- 22 fresh jalapeños
- 1lb. ground sage sausage
- 8 oz. cream cheese
- 1 cup freshly grated parmesan cheese

1. Preheat oven to 400.
2. Wash jalapeños.
3. Slice them in half length-wise and spoon out seeds and membranes.
4. Brown sausage in skillet and chop finely. Drain grease.
5. Add block of cream cheese and parmesan cheese.
6. Melt into sausage over low heat until combined.
7. Fill peppers with mixture and place in a baking dish.
8. Bake for 30 minutes uncovered.
9. Serve hot.

Makes 44
individual peppers

! CAUTION

Hi, my name is Chuck, I'm the designer of this cookbook. Shelley's cautionary tale above is NO JOKE, so I felt the need to make a special call-out box. I made these for a party recently, and even WITH the latex gloves, I could still feel the burn, although I didn't have to spend the night with my hands in ice water! But like she said, TOTALLY worth it. Seriously. People LOVED these things. **WEAR THE GLOVES.**

menu SUGGESTIONS

TACO BAR:
Shelley's Mom's Salsa with Chips
Katy's Low Fat Cheese Dip
Pulled Pork Tacos
Sopapilla Cheesecake (from Dessert chapter)

MEXICAN NIGHT AT THE BEACH:
Black Bean Everything served with chips
Guac Ohhhh Mole Hey served on a bed of shredded lettuce with diced tomato
Creamy Chicken Enchiladas
Blueberry Banana Dessert (from Dessert chapter)

CREAMY CHICKEN ENCHILADAS

from DENISE

For the last few years, we have tried hard to book our vacations at the same time for scheduling reasons and because we actually like each other enough to vacation at the same spot. Our favorite place is Rosemary Beach, FL. When more and more families began to join us for the week, we started getting together a couple of nights for a themed potluck dinner. I know you are not surprised that Mexican night has become a huge hit! Our friend Julie and Shelley made these chicken enchiladas last year and once again, the recipe came from Julie's sister, Betsy. If you want, you can join us in our pact to keep the secret ingredient a secret. (It's heavy cream, but no one needs to know, right?)

- 1 medium onion, chopped
- 1 T. butter
- 4 oz. can chopped green chiles
- 3½ cups cooked, diced chicken
- 8 oz. cream cheese
- ½ cup sour cream
- 10 (8 inch) flour tortillas
- 16 oz. shredded monterey jack cheese (not always available grated - you may have to buy a block and grate it yourself)
- 2 cups heavy cream

1. Preheat oven to 350.
2. Saute' onion in the butter in large skillet for 5 minutes on medium.
3. Add green chiles and saute' for 1 minute.
4. Stir in chicken and cream cheese.
5. Cook until the cream cheese melts, stirring constantly.
6. Stir in sour cream.
7. Spoon 2-3 T. of chicken mixture into each tortilla.
8. Arrange in lightly greased 9x13 pan.
9. Top with the monterey jack cheese and drizzle with the cream.
10. Bake for 30 to 45 minutes or until bubbly and light brown.

Serves 10-12

The beach gang...Adkisons, Borders, Joneses, Breens and Allmendingers (Shelley's sister!)

Why do I love Mexican food?
Two words: cilantro and cheese dip.
Okay so that's three words.
— SHELLEY

KATY'S LOW-FAT CHILI CHEESE DIP

from SHELLEY

Years ago, an incredibly talented Christian artist named Scott Krippayne entered the scene. Since his first big song, "Sometimes He Calms the Storm," we have absolutely loved his music. He has been on two of our "Winter Wonderland" Christmas tours as our special guest and was the opening act on our "I Choose You" tour. My husband David has also been Scott's booking agent for many years, so we became great friends with Scott and his awesome wife, Katy. Many years ago we had a Super Bowl party at our house and Katy walked in with a big crock pot of something yummy and cheesy looking. Turns out it was a delicious, low-fat cheese dip. I'm usually not a proponent of "low-fat" anything, but this is actually pretty darn good. Try it and see what you think!

- 1 large block of Velveeta Light Cheese
- 8 oz. fat free cream cheese
- 2 cans of turkey chili
- 1 can Ro-tel tomatoes

1. Melt cheese and cream cheese together in large pan over medium heat.
2. Add turkey chili and Ro-tel tomatoes.
3. Serve with tortilla chips.

Serves 10-12

Scott Krippayne and POG on the Christmas tour

MINI TACOS

from DENISE

One of our dreams when we moved to Nashville was to meet Michael W. Smith. Well, God arranged to give us even more than we dreamed of by allowing us to actually tour with him. We were able to go on three of his Christmas tours. While touring, we had the wonderful opportunity to meet Michael's sweet parents. His mom is an amazing cook and she has two cookbooks of her own. She was generous enough to give us each one of her cookbooks and to allow us to pass one of her signature recipes along to you! Everyone loves finger food and this is perfect for any type of party occasion.

- 1 lb. package egg-roll wrappers
- 1 lb. ground chuck, cooked, drained, and crumbled
- 1 package taco seasoning mix
- 16 oz. jar salsa
- 16 oz. package finely shredded cheddar cheese
- 8 oz. sour cream

1. Preheat oven to 350.
2. Remove wrappers from refrigerator 30 min. before cutting them.
3. With scissors, cut egg-roll wrappers across twice, horizontally and vertically to make 9 stacks. Then trim off edges.
4. Place wrappers in miniature muffin pans and bake for 5 minutes or until browned. (Note: they brown quickly.)
5. Mix ground chuck with taco seasoning and salsa.
6. Serve meat mixture in chafing dish, with the taco shells, cheese, and sour cream in bowls on the side.

smitty with Denise and shelley

(NOTE: The baked wrappers can be stored for a month in a closed container, or you can freeze them for several months. The meat for this dish can also be prepared in advance and frozen until ready for use.)

Makes 80 or more tacos

SOUTHWESTERN CHICKEN/CORN CHOWDER

from DENISE

Our friend Julie made this soup for us one chilly Halloween night. My husband Stu and I stopped by Shelley's house on the way home from trick-or-treating with our kids at another friend's house. OF COURSE, they had a whole spread of food and I couldn't resist having a plate. (Even though I had already had dinner and a ton of candy!) I tasted this Chicken/Corn Chowder and flipped out. No wonder it was disappearing faster than the candy! I told Julie right then that we had to add it to the cookbook. She said she got the recipe from her sister, Betsy, who is known for her excellent cooking. Their family makes it so often that they now refer to it as "The Soup."

- 3 cups cooked chicken breast, diced
- 3 pieces of bacon
- 3 T. butter
- 1 onion, diced
- ½ cup flour
- Two 14.5 oz cans chicken broth
- 28 oz. jar of salsa
- 16 oz. frozen white corn (thawed)
- 2 cups milk
- 2 T. cooking sherry
- grated sharp cheddar cheese for topping

1. Fry bacon in large pot.
2. Remove bacon and set aside (will use crumbled over soup later!)
3. Saute' onion in bacon grease and butter until onions are soft.
4. Add flour and stir until mixed well and starting to brown.
5. Add chicken broth, salsa, corn and chicken.
6. Simmer over low heat for 20 minutes.
7. Add milk and cooking sherry.
8. When soup heats back up it is ready to serve.
9. Serve topped with crumbled bacon and grated cheese

We also like to crumble tortilla chips or cornbread (or both) in it!

Serves 6-8

a quick POINT

Foods we find irresistible:

Shelley: I cannot say "no" to Mexican food. Ever.

Leigh: I cannot say "no" to sweets all together! I grew up eating dessert after every meal.

Denise: I cannot say "no" to chips, cheese dip and salsa!

MEXICAN CHILI

from LEIGH

This recipe came about thanks to my Aunt Wren and Shelley. I really like Shelley's bean chili and I love the tortilla soup that my Aunt Wren made one time on our "sisters" retreat in Asheville, NC. So one night I got a little crazy and decided to make my own chili concoction, and if I do say so myself it was "delicioso." It has now become a family favorite. We have to have it at least once a week. This is great for company too. You just put it in the Crockpot and enjoy your guests.

- 1 lb. lean ground beef
- 1 can light kidney beans
- 1 can dark kidney beans
- 1 can pinto beans
- 1 can of whole kernel corn
- 2 cans of Ro-tel tomatoes (I prefer mild instead of original)
- 1 pack of taco mild seasoning
- 1 pack of ranch dressing seasoning
- 1 can of beer (Don't let this freak you out, the alcohol is cooked out)

1. Brown ground beef and drain grease.
2. Drain all beans and corn (except pintos).
3. Place all ingredients in Crockpot on med/high.
4. Let sit in Crockpot for at least 2 hours.
5. Serve with a dollop of sour cream and shredded cheese on top with some tortilla chips - FANTASTICO!!!

Serves 4-6

BLACK BEAN EVERYTHING

from SHELLEY

I have always loved this wonderfully chunky dip my mom makes. I can see her biggest white Tupperware bowl filled with this yummy stuff right now! It's also very healthy, with no added oils or sugars. She usually makes up a batch when we are at the beach in the summer. It's a great afternoon snack with tortilla chips, but we also found it to be a wonderful topping for fish or chicken. Tired of the usual green salad? Throw in a couple spoons of Black Bean Everything! You will love this versatile dish!

- 3 cans of black beans, rinsed and drained
- 1 can white shoe peg corn, drained
- 2 cans of Ro-tel tomotoes
- 1 bunch of green onions, chopped
- 3 red peppers, chopped
- 2 cups of chopped tomatoes
- 1 cup chopped cilantro
- ¼ cup of red wine vinegar
- juice of one lemon
- cumin to taste
- 1 clove of minced garlic
- chili powder and cayenne pepper to taste
- 1 chopped jalapeño

1. In large bowl combine black beans, corn, Ro-tel tomatoes, green onions, red peppers, tomatoes and cilantro.
2. In small bowl mix red wine vinegar, lemon juice, cumin, garlic, chili powder, cayenne pepper and jalapeño. (Adjust spices to your taste!)
3. Add to remaining ingredients and chill in refrigerator. Makes a very large bowl!
4. Serve with corn chips or on top of chicken or fish. Also excellent mixed into a green salad. This has many uses and can last you all week!

Serves 12-14

KING RANCH CASSEROLE

from DENISE

When Point of Grace moved to Nashville, we met an amazing woman named Nancy Alcorn who had begun an incredible ministry for troubled young women called "Mercy Ministries of America." We were singing in Monroe, LA where their very first home for girls was located. Nancy invited us to come and visit while we were in town. I will never forget that day. We walked in the door and were greeted by hugs and smiles from about 20 girls. They had spent the morning preparing a home-cooked meal for us. The main dish was King Ranch Casserole. Looking at these young ladies, you would never guess their stories. After an amazing lunch, we were able to just sit around and talk. Each girl shared with us why they were there. It was everything from abuse to eating disorders to unplanned pregnancy. However, the joy on their faces explained the transformation that only God can do in someone's life. Every time I make this meal I think of these girls and how God continues to heal the brokenhearted through this ministry. "Mercy Ministries" has now turned into an International ministry with homes all over the world. I thank God for women like Nancy who step out in faith to what God has called them to do. **(To learn more information about Mercy Ministries go to www.mercyministries.org.)**

- 6 pieces of boneless, skinless chicken breast, cooked and cut up
- ½ stick butter
- 1 onion, chopped
- 16 oz. can diced tomatoes
- 8 oz. American cheese
- ½ cup chicken broth (from boiling the chicken)
- ½ t. garlic powder
- ½ t. chili powder
- 8 oz. mild cheddar cheese, grated
- crushed tortilla chips to make ½ inch layer in bottom of 9x13 baking dish
- 1 can cream of mushroom soup
- 1 can cream of chicken soup

Our dear friend Nancy Alcorn and POG

1. Preheat oven to 350.
2. Grease 9x13 baking dish.
3. Crush chips in bottom of baking dish.
4. Saute onion in butter.
5. In large bowl combine all ingredients except cheddar cheese.
6. Pour mixture over chips.
7. Top with cheddar cheese.
8. Bake for 30 minutes or until bubbly.

Serves 8-10

PULLED PORK TACOS

from SHELLEY

Okay, these tacos are just plain awesome! Whenever the neighbors have a big Crockpot of these cooking, I just go ahead and invite myself over. I will admit they are a little work: preparing the meat with a rub the night before, cooking for several hours in the oven the following day, then shredding and transferring to the Crockpot for final touches! But I promise, the minute you taste them it will be worth all the effort. Many thanks again to Mr. Rob, our neighbor, cook and friend, for sharing his secrets!

- 6 lb. pork butt
- 2 T. hot Mexican-style chili powder
- 2 T. garlic salt
- 2 T. cumin
- 1 can Ro-tel tomatoes (drained)
- 1 cup medium salsa
- 1 T. cumin
- 1 T. hot Mexican-style chili powder
- 1 T. garlic salt
- 1 t. salt
- 1 t. pepper
- 1 T. hot sauce
- ½ t. cayenne pepper

1. Rub pork generously with hot Mexican-style chili powder, garlic salt and cumin.
2. Cover with plastic wrap.
4. Chill overnight.
5. Cover with foil and cook for six hours at 300 degrees.
6. Trim fat and shred. Place shredded pork in slow cooker and add ingredients from Ro-tel through cayenne pepper.
6. Cook on low for two hours.

Serve on flour tortillas with shredded cheese, lettuce, sour cream and salsa.

Serves 18-20 (or more - so invite lots of friends!)

OUR FAVORITE MEXICAN RESTAURANTS!

1. LUPE TORTILLA - This is in Houston, Texas. They have the best beef fajitas we have ever put in our mouths. We don't know what's in the marinade, but it is RIDICULOUSLY good. We could eat two pounds of that meat like it is candy. And to top it off, the tortillas are the size of hubcaps!

2. LAS PALMAS - There are many locations all over Nashville and we have been to most of them. We love their white cheese dip, salsa, pico de gallo, and ESPECIALLY their chicken chimichangas! Fried cheesy goodness! Oh, they do have chicken in them, too.

3. GARCIA'S - This is located in Franklin, Tennessee. It's one of those strip mall Mexican joints, but a step above. We love, love, love their salsa. They also have this thing called Quesadilla Garcia. It's a chorizo sausage quesadilla with some kind of creamy, spicy sauce that is sooooooo good. Sometimes a couple of us will split one….that way we can eat five baskets of chips!

4. PAPACITA'S – This restaurant is in Longview, Texas. This is FANTASTIC Mexican Food. The tortillas are puffy like a piece of bread!

5. EL TORERO – It's located in Stone Mountain, Georgia. When we were on the "Come Alive Tour," the hotel clerk recommended it to us and you just never know how that will pan out. Well, this guy was right on the money. Their Sunday brunch was a festive feast full of flavor (say that 5 times fast)!

MEXICAN CORNBREAD

from LEIGH

As you know, cornmeal can have many uses. It's not just a southern thang. My daddy makes a great Mexican cornbread! It has quite the kick. I love Mexican food and when I am not in the mood to leave the house for our favorite Mexican restaurant, this is my close second: Daddy's Mexican cornbread, a bowl of my chili, our favorite DVD and a cozy fire. Muy bueno!

- 1½ cups cornmeal
- 1 cup flour
- 1½ cups grated cheddar cheese
- 1 cup buttermilk
- ½ cup vegetable oil
- 1 onion, chopped
- 2 eggs
- 2-4 jalapeño peppers, chopped (according to your taste)
- 1 large can cream style corn
- 1 green or red bell pepper, chopped

1. Preheat oven to 425.
2. Mix all ingredients together.
3. Pour into greased 9x13 baking dish.
4. Bake for 30-35 minutes.

This is so good and believe it or not, kids love it!

Serves 8-10

Mi papa

CHAPTER EIGHT

SO, YOU HAVE A SWEET TOOTH...

DESSERT

If we didn't know better, it would seem like the purpose of our POG tours is to experience new, tasty, chewy, yummy treats! We love to try out recipes on each other and what better place to share our creations than on the bus? Then, when we arrive at churches or other venues, there is often a whole spread of goodies at catering and in our dressing rooms. Our fans sure do know the way to our hearts! Ah, so many sweets, so little time!

GLAZED TEA CAKE

from SHELLEY

Seriously, this cake is so good that when my friend Julie made it for my birthday last year I had to call her after the party and 'fess up that I had eaten the scraps off of people's plates as I was cleaning up! (I just couldn't let even a bite go to waste, now could I?) The true test, however, is that our friend Jill, who doesn't even like cake, requested it for her birthday this year…at two separate celebrations!

Tea Cake:
- 2 cups flour
- 2 cups sugar
- 1 t. salt
- 1 t. baking powder
- 1 cup butter
- 1 cup water
- ½ cup sour cream
- 2 large eggs
- 1 t. almond extract

DOUGH OR DIE

POG ON EATING RAW COOKIE DOUGH AND/OR CAKE BATTER:

LEIGH: I only eat the cake batter - cookie dough doesn't do it for me.

SHELLEY: HECK YES I eat the raw cookie dough…and cake batter….whatever…I don't give a second thought to the raw eggs!

DENISE: I eat both for sure!

1. Preheat oven to 350.
2. Grease and flour a ½ sheet cake pan (approx. 18x12 inches).
3. In a large bowl, combine flour, sugar, salt and baking powder. Set aside.
4. In a small saucepan, combine butter and water. Bring to a boil, stirring occasionally.
5. Add to flour mixture, stirring to combine. Stir in sour cream, eggs and almond extract.
6. Pour into prepared pan and bake for 22-25 minutes.
7. Let cake cool and then pour on the Tea Cake Glaze.

Tea Cake Glaze:
- ½ cup butter
- ¼ cup milk
- ½ t. almond extract
- 3 cups powdered sugar

1. In a medium saucepan, combine butter and milk.
2. Bring to a boil over medium heat, stirring occasionally.
3. Remove from heat.
4. Whisk in almond extract.
5. Gradually whisk in powdered sugar until smooth.
6. Spread over tea cake.
7. Cut into squares and serve.

Serving idea: Julie's sister Betsy decorates each square with butter cream frosting squeezed from a pastry bag. Guests at wedding and baby showers often ask her where she buys the beautiful petit fours!

Serves 20+

EASY BREEZY CHOCOLATE BUNDT CAKE

from DENISE

When my husband Stu and I moved into our first house, we had three families who lived all around us and we became very close. To this day, they are still some of our closest friends and I don't know how we would get through life without them. Through the years we have celebrated many occasions: birthdays, graduations, baptisms, anniversaries, etc. All of them usually require some kind of food. This particular chocolate cake is one of my very favorites. When my neighbor Lori Brown first made it, I thought that it must have been super hard. She laughed and told me how easy it was. See for yourself!

- 1 box chocolate cake mix
- 1 small box instant chocolate pudding
- 8 oz. sour cream
- 3 eggs
- ¾ cup oil
- ¾ cup water
- 1 t. vanilla
- 8 oz. chocolate chips

1. Preheat oven to 350.
2. Mix all ingredients together (except for chocolate chips) in a mixing bowl 'til smooth and creamy.
3. Add in the chocolate chips.
4. Pour into greased bundt pan.
5. Bake for 50 to 60 min. on middle rack (I usually check mine at about 40 to 45 minutes because my oven seems to cook faster.)
6. If you want to, you can serve it with heated chocolate sauce or just sprinkle a little powdered sugar on it for looks.

Serves 10-12

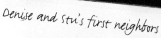

Denise and Stu's first neighbors

AUNT DOROTHY'S FROSTING CAKE

from SHELLEY

I can barely write about my Great Aunt Dorothy without getting a little teary-eyed. She was the closest thing to an angel here on Earth that existed in my family. All of my relatives would quickly agree with that statement. She was like a second mother to my dad, my Uncle Jesse and my Aunt Sandi when they were growing up. She was absolutely the epitome of "salt of the earth." She passed away only about a year ago, but her memory will live on in all of our hearts.

She was an incredible cook and could turn out huge southern style meals in her tiny little kitchen there in North Little Rock. She was famous for a lot of things in our family: yeast rolls, chicken and dumplings, you name it! But some of my favorite things she made were her desserts. I remember sitting at her table after a meal one night eating a piece of delectable pound cake. I asked her for the recipe and she told me the secret to the cake's moistness was a can of ready-made frosting! So I have always just called this "Aunt Dorothy's Frosting Cake."

I could go on and on about her cooking, but it wouldn't hold a candle to the stories we all have about how she helped, served, prayed for and cared for each of us with a gentleness and sweetness that was in a class all by itself. I always said if I had a second little girl, her name would be Dorothy. Well, that's not likely to happen at this point, but nonetheless, Aunt Dorothy's memory and legacy made a huge mark on all of us. She would be so thrilled to know her recipe was in this cookbook because nothing made her happier than to cook for people she loved.

- 1 box yellow cake mix
- 4 eggs
- 1 cup of vegetable oil
- 1 cup water
- 1 can creamy deluxe coconut pecan frosting
- ½ cup chopped pecans

1. Preheat oven to 350.
2. Combine first four ingredients and mix well with electric mixer.
3. Fold in frosting and stir well.
4. Grease and flour a bundt pan.
5. Pour in cake mixture.
6. Bake on middle rack (you don't want the bottom to burn!) of oven for 45-60 minutes.
7. Remove from pan while hot.

Serves 10-12

Caroline, Aunt Dorothy, Grant and Shelley's sister Robyn

BEST CHOCOLATE PIE EVER

from LEIGH

Growing up, my Mom made this Chocolate Pie that was creamy and delicious!!! NO one knew the recipe and we were too afraid to ask. Last Christmas, my mom surprised my sisters and me with the secret recipe, as well as the proper cookware! (It was the best gift ever according to my daughter.) Now I get the "wow" at dinner parties when I bring my Mom's famous and VERY easy chocolate pie. Her secret is out and I'm so glad that the WORLD can enjoy what I consider the best chocolate pie ever!

- 2 Graham cracker crusts
- 2 cups sugar
- ½ cup all purpose flour
- ⅔ cup cocoa
- pinch salt
- 4 egg yolks
- 4 cups milk
- 2 t. vanilla

1. Measure dry ingredients and stir together until blended.
2. Separate egg yolks and egg whites. (See Cooking Class in Side Dishes)
3. Add 4 cups milk, beaten egg yolks and vanilla flavoring to dry mixture.
4. Heat in microwave on high in 2 minute increments.
5. Stir after each 2 minutes.
6. When thickened to right consistency (thick and creamy) pour into pie crusts.
7. Cool, then top with whipped cream.

Serves 16
(makes 2 pies)

Every good chef needs a good helper.

Leigh's finished product

JOJO'S HOT FUDGE SUNDAE CAKE

from DENISE

Jojo is my friend Kelley's mom. Of course that's not her real name but that's what all the grandkids call her. She is one of those people who never meets a stranger and has made us feel like we are part of their family. A few years ago we began a tradition of going to Jojo's house in Pulaski, TN on Good Friday. Easter is her favorite time of year. She lives out on some beautiful property and all of the kids get to play baseball, football and have a huge Easter egg hunt, but not before Jojo shares the Easter story with them. We all bring lots of different dishes to eat, but this is one of Jojo's specialties.

- 1 cup flour
- ¾ cup sugar
- 2 T. cocoa
- 2 t. baking powder
- ¼ teaspoon salt
- ½ cup milk
- 2 T. oil
- 1 t. vanilla
- 1 cup chopped nuts
- 1 cup brown sugar, packed
- ¼ cup cocoa
- 1¾ cup hottest tap water
- vanilla ice cream

Jojo and the grandkids

1. Preheat oven to 350.
2. Stir together flour, granulated sugar, 2 T. cocoa, baking powder, and salt in an ungreased 9x9x2 square pan.
3. Mix in milk, oil, vanilla with fork 'til smooth.
4. Stir in nuts.
5. Sprinkle with brown sugar and ¼ cup cocoa. Pour hot water over batter. Bake 40 minutes at 350 degrees. Let stand 15 min. Spoon into dishes-top with ice cream!!!

Serves 6-8

AIRPLANE'S BEST HOT FUDGE SAUCE

from SHELLEY

No, this is not the hot fudge that you sometimes get in first class on long Delta flights. (Though I must say, those sundaes they serve you at 35,000 feet are pretty darn good!) My friend Jill is sorta like my husband Dave in that she grew up in Michigan and her parents still live there. They were down for a visit when my daughter was probably only 3 three years old. I introduced Caroline to Jill's mom, Miss Elaine, to which she promptly responded, "Hi Airplane." It was really cute and the name sorta stuck.

A little known fact that I will just throw in here is that my daughter also has a crazy nickname that has stuck since she was a baby. Our closest friends and my parents still call her this and she has never questioned it, not once. Anyway, I made up this little song that I sang to her when she was a baby...."Kooky, kooky Caroline Breen, the cutest girl that I've seen..." And ever since then, she has been known as "The Kooks." (Pronounced with the same vowel as "shoot".) I know, I know, doesn't that sound weird and even kinda mean?! She really isn't weird or "kooky," never was actually, but every time I talk to Jill, she asks how "the kooks" is!

Anyway, back to Airplane's hot fudge sauce. It just takes a little extra time to make this topping for your ice cream, but it is SO worth it! I finally wrote the recipe down one time and have been making it ever since. In fact, I own a double boiler now solely because of this recipe. It's rich and creamy and so much better than what you find in the jar!

- ½ stick of butter
- 2 squares of Baker's semi-sweet chocolate
- 1 ½ cups sugar
- 1 t. vanilla
- ¾ cup evaporated milk

1. In a double boiler, melt butter and chocolate squares.
2. Slowly stir in the sugar until it is dissolved.
3. Add vanilla and milk, stirring until smooth.

Will keep refrigerated for up to two weeks.

SNICKERS SALAD

from DENISE

Who in the world wouldn't want to eat a salad made with snickers?! Seriously, whoever invented it was a genius. I make this salad every Easter and it is always a big hit. In fact, it is SUCH a hit that I usually have to make a double recipe!

- 8 oz. cream cheese, softened
- 7 oz. jar marshmallow cream
- 1 small tub whipped cream, thawed
- 1 bag of miniature Snickers, quartered
- 1 ½ Granny smith apples, cubed

1. Combine cream cheese and marshmallow cream.
2. Add whipped cream.
3. Stir in Snickers and apples.
4. Keep refrigerated.

Serves 6-8

COOKING CLASS #8

WE'RE GETTING CRUSTY: In this day and age of ready-made everything, making your own crust is becoming a lost art. By all means, if you are in a hurry, buy a frozen or refrigerated crust for your pie. If you are feeling adventurous and would like a taste of how they did it "back in the day," then follow the tips below:

A. The right tools are important! We suggest: a pastry blender, a good rolling pin (a heavy, marble one is best) and good pie plates (pans).

B. You need a good recipe! The one from Denise's grandmother (with Coconut Cream Pie) is perfect! Let's walk through her recipe together: Our words are in BLUE.

PASTRY CRUST RECIPE
- 1 cup flour • ½ t. salt • ⅓ cup plus 1 T. shortening • 4 T. water
1. Sift flour and salt together.
2. Cut in shortening with a pastry blender or knives and work it 'til it is blended together. "Cut in" means to stir using cutting motions – this used to be done with 2 knives cutting through mixture in opposite directions. Nowadays, the pastry blender is easier to use.
3. Add the water and form into a ball. Put some flour on your hands first before forming the ball. Roll dough around in your hands.
4. Flatten on a floured surface and roll from center to the edge until 1/8 inch thick. Flour liberally! Put it on your hands, all over the counter top, on your dough and keep re-applying to your rolling pin. You want it to end up round.
5. Place in pie pan and flute the edges. Fluting means to press your fingers or a fork all the way around the edge of the crust. This will hold it in place as well as make it look pretty. At this point, you may want to take a knife and run it along the outer edge of pie plate to remove any excess, uneven dough.
6. Prick bottom and sides of crust well with fork. This helps to give the crust a flaky texture by letting air into the dough.
7. Bake at 400 degrees until crust is a light golden brown (about 15 minutes).

C. You also will need a little bit of patience! It is frustrating when the dough tears or sticks to the rolling pin. It takes practice to learn exactly how much flour you need to keep this from happening. If your dough tears while you are transferring it to the pie plate, just mash it back together with your fingers and proceed. Don't worry, your family won't mind if you practice your pie making skills on them!

PECAN PIE

from LEIGH

You can't live on a pecan orchard and NOT know how to make a mouth watering pecan pie. My Granddaddy knew it well and actually, the whole Ivester clan knows, thanks to him. Traditionally, we served the pie alone. (No ice cream on top as it was uncommon for us to have ice cream in the freezer. We churned homemade.) Anyway, my favorite way to serve pecan pie currently is with vanilla ice cream on top then drizzled with chocolate syrup. I think Granddaddy would approve.

- 1 box light brown sugar
- 1 stick margarine, melted
- 4 eggs
- 2 T. corn meal
- 2 T. water
- 1 T. vanilla
- pinch of salt
- 2 cups of pecans, broken
- 2 frozen, unbaked pie shells

1. Preheat oven to 325.
2. Beat eggs and add other ingredients.
3. Mix together well and pour equally into pie shells.
4. Bake for 45 minutes or more. *(Tip: Pie is done when center reaches 200 degrees. Tap center of pie lightly with your finger. If pie is done it should "spring" back. Place foil strip around edges to keep edges from over-browning.)*

Serves 12-16
(makes 2 pies)

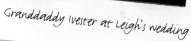
Granddaddy Ivester at Leigh's wedding

SOPAPILLA CHEESECAKE

from SHELLEY

Thirteen years ago when David and I got married, we bought a little house on a quiet street that was sort of a "fixer upper," and I guess we just assumed that we wouldn't live there too long. We fell in love with the neighborhood and the location, but mostly, our neighbors. Rob and Kirsten Howard have three children: Caleb, Sarah and Ben. They are truly like brothers and sisters to Caroline, which is important since she is an only child! We call one another "Framily," which is Kirsten's little word for "friends that are like family" and I guess that's about as accurate of a description of our relationship as any. We have shared so much through the years, but probably the thing we have shared the most is food. Literally. They are my taste testers for new recipes and are always willing to take our leftovers. It's kinda nice for me to know that my food never goes to waste. I just bring it to the Howard's. They're kinda like Mikey. They'll eat anything! Kirsten has many talents, but she would tell you herself that cooking is not one of them. I will tell you this, she can flat out tear it up if you need something creative done. She's a master at graphic design. I have the most "over the top," cool Christmas cards every year because of her. I look just like I do on my record covers, which is a much better version of myself, because she is a master "photo-shopper!" Just don't ask her to follow a recipe! Rob and I would be the cooks of the "framily," but Kirsten does have a few "famous" standbys that she makes when she's not designing a record cover (or her neighbor's Christmas card.) This is one of my favorites. It's so good served hot with vanilla ice cream and it's super simple to put together! Enjoy it with your friends or your family or your "framily"...

- 2 cans of refrigerated crescent rolls
- 8 oz. cream cheese, softened
- 1 stick of margarine
- 2 cups sugar (divided use)
- cinnamon
- 1 tsp. of vanilla

1. Preheat oven to 350.
2. Press one can of crescent rolls (leave the dough connected) in the bottom of a greased 9 x 13 baking dish.
3. Stretch the dough and seal to cover the bottom of the pan.
4. Mix cream cheese, vanilla, and one cup of sugar together.
5. Spread mixture on top of crescent dough.
6. Cover mixture with the second can of crescent dough.
7. Melt margarine and remaining 1 cup sugar together in a saucepan over medium heat. Pour mixture over top and sprinkle with cinnamon.
8. Bake for 30 minutes or until top is golden brown. Serve warm.

Serves 12-15

The Breens with the Howards, minus Kirsten (above), who was taking the picture!

PAM'S CARAMEL FILLED CHOCOLATE COOKIES

from DENISE

One of the best things about women's Bible studies is that you usually get to taste incredible food. It makes me dream about the banquet table that the Lord is preparing for us and it is going to be fat free! Woo Hoo! This cookie is definitely not fat free, but it sure is good. The only problem for me is that I don't ever make it because it takes too long. So if we ever have these on the bus it will be because Shelley decided to make them. However, I can promise you it is worth the time…and calories! What could be better than a chocolate cookie with a Rolo in it?

- 2¼ cup flour
- ¾ cup unsweetened cocoa
- 1 t. baking soda
- 1 cup sugar
- 1 cup brown sugar
- 1 cup butter or margarine, softened
- 2 t. vanilla
- 2 eggs
- 1 cup pecans, chopped
- 48 Rolos (1 pkg)
- 1 T. sugar

1. Preheat oven to 375.
2. In large bowl beat 1 cup sugar, brown sugar and butter until fluffy.
3. Add vanilla and eggs, beat well.
4. Add flour, cocoa and baking soda. Blend well.
5. Stir in ½ cup pecans.
6. For each cookie, shape about 1 T. of dough around the Rolo, covering it completely.
7. In small bowl combine remaining ½ cup pecans and 1 T. sugar.
8. Press one side of each ball into pecan mixture.
9. Place nut side up 2 inches apart on un-greased cookie sheet.
10. Bake for 7 to 10 minutes
11. Let cool 2 minutes.
12. Remove from sheet and cool completely.
13. You can drizzle chocolate over them if you want.

Note: They freeze great.

Makes 4 dozen

Dessert is one of my four basic food groups.
(I took out vegetables.)
— SHELLEY

CHOCOLATE SCOTCHEROOS

from SHELLEY

I think one of the neatest gifts I have ever received was from my mother-in-law Veronica. She lives in Michigan and we don't get to see her as much as we'd like, but she and I share a love of great food! I can't remember if it was for Christmas or my birthday or maybe some other occasion, but she gave me a cute little recipe box that I just loved. I still have it and it is where I keep my treasure chest of my very favorite things to cook. The best part was not the box, but what was inside it. She had included several of David's favorite recipes from growing up and some of the things she considers her yummiest standbys, all written out on matching recipe cards in her own writing. I had trouble deciding which one to include, but these are really great little cookie bars that are easy and delicious and I thought they might be perfect for our dessert chapter. I hope you enjoy this little Michigan treasure!

- 1 cup corn syrup
- 1 cup sugar
- 1 cup peanut butter
- 6 cups of crisp rice cereal
- 1 cup semi-sweet chocolate chips
- 1 cup butterscotch chips

1. In large saucepan cook corn syrup and sugar over medium heat, stirring frequently, until mixture begins to boil.
2. Remove from heat. Stir in peanut butter, then mix in cereal.
3. Press into buttered 13 x 9 pan.
4. Melt chocolate and butterscotch chips in a double boiler, stirring constantly until smooth.
5. Spread over cereal mixture.
6. Chill until firm and cut into squares to serve.

Makes about 15

Grandma Veronica and Caroline in the Michigan snow

JULIE'S NEW & IMPROVED CHOCOLATE CHIP COOKIES

from LEIGH

Julie says this recipe evolved over the years as a result of her quest to perfect her chocolate chip cookies. She didn't like the way they would sometimes turn out "cakey." When she brought these cookies to us on the bus recently, I couldn't believe the chewy texture they had. They were downright gourmet. She said there are some secrets to this recipe, but she did agree to let us put it in our cookbook. I guess those secrets aren't so secret anymore, honey!

- 1 cup. butter flavored shortening
- ¾ cup brown sugar, packed
- ¾ cup sugar
- 1 egg
- 1 t. vanilla
- 2¼ cups flour
- 1 t. salt
- 1 t. baking soda
- 1½ T. milk
- 10 oz. chocolate chips
- ½ cup chopped pecans (optional)

(Secret #1: all mixing will be done by hand. Julie says that electric mixers put too much air into the batter, which produces a "cakey" texture.)

Leigh, Julie, Denise and Shelley

1. Preheat oven to 350.
2. In large bowl, cream shortening and sugars together by hand until well mixed. (Secret #2: butter flavored shortening has a better consistency than butter, and is tastier than regular shortening.)
3. Add vanilla and egg and continue mixing by hand. (Secret #3: less egg than traditional recipe for a chewier texture.)
4. Add flour mixture – a little at a time (dough will be stiff) and mix well.
5. Add milk and mix well.
6. Mix in chocolate chips and nuts.
7. Drop by teaspoonfuls onto un-greased cookie sheet – 1½ inches apart.
8. Bake for 10-12 minutes – or until just starting to brown on top.
9. Remove from oven and let cool for 5 minutes. (Secret #4: this is very important – cookies will crumble if you don't let them cool for a few minutes before removing from cookie sheet.)
10. Remove cookies from sheet and continue cooling on wire rack.

Makes 3-4 dozen

CREAM PUFFS

from LEIGH

Please don't make me cook certain things! Once upon a time, my husband Dana had my friend and neighbor Peggy's cream puffs. That was all he talked about for months. He wanted more. I wondered if I could make his dream come true. His birthday was just around the corner so I wanted my gift to Dana to be yummy cream puffs. I was too afraid to go it alone, so Peggy was kind enough to help me step by step. (Really she did it all and I just stirred the pudding.) Dana was thrilled with his delicious gift, but I haven't had the courage to make them again. We will all live happily ever after, though, because Peggy invites us over whenever she makes them!

Cream Puff Paste (for shell):
- 1 cup water
- ½ cup butter or margarine
- 1 cup all purpose flour
- ⅛ tsp salt
- 4 large eggs

Dana and Peggy

1. Preheat oven to 400.
2. Combine water and butter in a medium saucepan; bring to a boil.
3. Add flour and salt all at once, stirring vigorously over medium-high heat until mixture leaves sides of pan and forms a smooth ball. Remove from heat, and cool 4-5 min.
4. Add eggs, one at a time, beating thoroughly with a wooden spoon after each addition. Beat until dough is smooth.
5. Drop by tablespoonfuls onto baking sheet 3 inches apart. Bake at 400 for 20-25 min or until golden and puffed up.
6. After cooling, cut top off of each cream puff; pull out insides and discard soft dough inside.
7. Fill bottom halves with cream filling and cover with the top half.
8. Drizzle with your favorite bottled chocolate sauce. (Or use Airplane's best! See page 153.)

(cont. next page)

Cream Puff Filling:

- 5 egg yolks
- ½ cup sugar
- ⅓ cup all purpose flour
- 2 cups milk
- 1 T. butter
- 2 t. vanilla

1. Combine egg yolks and sugar in a heavy saucepan, stirring with a wire whisk until smooth.
2. Add flour, and stir until blended; gradually stir in milk.
3. Cook over medium heat, stirring constantly. (Mixture will appear to curdle; continue to sir and it will become smooth.)
4. Reduce heat to medium-low when mixture thickens and begins to bubble.
5. Continue to cook 3 more minutes, stirring constantly.
6. Cool to lukewarm; stir in butter and vanilla.
7. Cover and chill 2 hours.

Makes 2-3 dozen

ELAINE'S ICE CREAM PIE

from SHELLEY

If you haven't figured it out yet, Elaine and Airplane are the same person. You will have to read the Hot Fudge Story to see why! I will never forget the first time I ever ate this ice cream pie. It was love at first bite. We were at my friend Jill's house on a Monday night, at our weekly "Bachelorette" watching party. In my opinion, this is one of the greatest shows on television. I have watched every single episode of the "Bachelor" and "Bachelorette" on ABC and I am not ashamed to say it. It's television at its finest. There are a few people in my life (VERY few) who share my opinion of this show. Most people just make fun of me, but I am confident in my beliefs and I do not care what others say! So, every Monday night, (and I might add, it's our favorite night of the week) we gather to watch the love story unfold. Of course, delicious food is always on the agenda, as well. Because I know Elaine would be honored, I would like to dedicate this recipe to our little Monday night group: Marcia, Chuck, Sarah (aka Miss McGarry), Jessie, Julie and Jill. We are an eclectic bunch for sure, but like I said, Monday is now our favorite night of the week because we have so much fun. It's worth noting, however, that no one else is allowed into the fold. There just simply wouldn't be enough ice cream pie!

- 1 stick butter, melted
- ¼ cup brown sugar, packed
- 1 cup flour
- ½ cup pecans, chopped
- Half gallon of your favorite ice cream
- ¾ jar caramel ice cream sauce

1. Preheat oven to 400.
2. Mix sugar and flour and add nuts.
3. Pour melted butter over this.
4. Spread thin on cookie sheet with fingers.
5. Bake 8-10 minutes until light brown. Don't over-bake.
6. Remove from oven and put crust into bowl and crumble.
7. Save ¾ cup of crumbs for top of pie.
8. Press into a buttered pie plate.
9. Drizzle ¼ jar caramel sauce carefully over crust (before you put ice cream in).
10. Freeze at least 45 min.
11. Soften ice cream (any kind) just so it spreads easily in the piecrust.
12. Pile it as high as you wish.
13. Sprinkle reserved crumbs on top of pie and drizzle another ½ cup of caramel sauce over all of pie.
14. Freeze 1-2 hours or longer.
15. Remove from freezer 5 min. before serving.

Jill, Elaine (Airplane), Sharon and Shelley

You can vary this by using an oreo-type cookie crust (in the baking aisle).

Serves 8-10

CHERRY DELIGHT

from DENISE

When I think of "sweet," I can't help but think of my sister Donita. There is not a sweeter person in the world. She is one of those people that truly delights herself in the Lord and therefore brings joy to those around her. In fact, she makes this dessert for my Mom most every Christmas because it's her favorite. It's creamy and light, yet rich and delicious all in the same bite. For all of the cherry lovers out there, you won't be disappointed!

- 1½ sticks butter, softened
- 1½ cups flour
- 2 T. granulated sugar
- 1 cup pecans, finely chopped
- 1 t. vanilla
- 8 oz. cream cheese, softened
- 2 cups powdered sugar
- Two 21 oz. cans cherry pie filling
- 8 oz. whipped cream

Denise and Donita at Denise's wedding.

1. Preheat oven to 350.
2. Cream butter, flour, pecans and sugar together to make crust.
3. Press crust mixture into bottom of a 9x13 pan. Bake for 20 minutes. Let cool completely.
4. While crust is baking, mix together vanilla, cream cheese and powdered sugar, then spread over cooled crust.
5. Spread cherry pie filling over cream cheese layer.
6. We serve it with a dollop of whipped cream on top to make it pretty.

Serves 12-15

COCONUT CREAM PIE

from DENISE

Grandmother Daisy (we called her "Ma") and her sister, my Great Aunt Mildred made the best from scratch cream pies in the whole wide world. To this day, if Aunt Mildred doesn't bring her pies to the church functions, people actually get upset. I grew up watching "Ma" make pies. She made it look so easy, but there was only one problem. When it came time for me to get married and I asked her to help me learn to make a few things, it didn't turn out so well. She had it all in her head, but couldn't ever sit down and write out exact measurements. So, I never learned how to make those pies. Well, Aunt Mildred has come to the rescue by giving me her secrets! I'm sharing with you the Coconut Cream Pie, but at the end of the recipe I am giving you optional ways to make pineapple cream, banana cream, butterscotch cream and chocolate cream. You can become a great pie maker too. The next time there is a bake sale, people will be placing their orders!

Pastry Crust:
- 1 cup flour
- ½ t. salt
- ⅓ cup plus 1 T. shortening
- 4 T. water

1. Sift flour and salt together.
2. Cut in shortening with a pastry blender or knives and work it 'til it is blended together.
3. Add the water and form into a ball.
4. Flatten on a floured surface and roll from center to the edge until ⅛ inch thick.
5. Place in pie pan and flute the edges.
6. Prick bottom and sides of crust well with fork.
7. Bake at 400 degrees until crust is a light golden brown, then set aside.

Filling:
- 1 cup sugar
- ½ cup flour
- ⅛ t. salt
- 3 cups whole milk
- 3 egg yolks (save the whites for the meringue)
- 4 T. margarine
- 1 T. imitation vanilla
  (Aunt Mildred likes the taste of it better than the real vanilla.)
- ¾ cup grated coconut

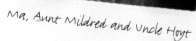
Ma, Aunt Mildred and Uncle Hoyt

1. Put sugar, flour and salt in top of double boiler. Stir with spoon to mix well.
2. Stir in ½ cup milk and mix well. (I suggest using a whisk.)
3. Add egg yolk and stir vigorously to make a paste.
4. Add remaining milk, stir well.
5. Cook over boiling water in the double boiler stirring frequently with wisk.
6. Cook until thick
7. Add margarine and vanilla and stir until margarine melts.
8. Add coconut and stir well.
9. Set aside while making meringue

(cont. next page)

Meringue:
- 3 egg whites
- 1 T. imitation vanilla
- ⅛ t. cream of tarter
- 1 t. cold water
- ¼ cup sugar

1. Mix all ingredients except for sugar in a mixing bowl.
2. Beat until stiff.
3. Add sugar and continue beating until stiff and glassy peaks form.

Assemble the pie:
1. Put pie filling in shell and spread meringue on top. (Make sure to seal the meringue on to the edge of crust or it will pull away when cooking.)
2. Sprinkle a little extra coconut on top of meringue.
3. Bake at 25-35 minutes or until golden brown.

Serves 6-8

VARIATIONS
Pineapple Cream: In the filling, replace coconut with ¾ cup crushed pineapple.
Banana Cream: Slice 2 large bananas and sprinkle with lemon juice to keep from turning brown. Lay the bananas on the baked crust then put filling on top of bananas.
Butterscotch Cream: Replace sugar in filling with 1 cup and 3 T. of brown sugar
Chocolate Cream: Add 4 T. cocoa to the filling by sifting it into the sugar, flour, and salt mixture in step 1 of the filling. Make sure to continue to stir so that cocoa won't get lumpy.

BETTER THAN "YOU KNOW WHAT" CAKE 2

from SHELLEY

We really went back and forth on whether or not to include this recipe in our cookbook. Not because it's not delicious, but because the actual name contained that little three letter word that is sometimes taboo in Christian circles...thus, the name change. I mean, I find it hilarious that we can't print THAT word- because without stating the obvious, we DO all have children! But in an effort not to offend anyone, yada yada... I have absolutely no recollection as to where I got this recipe, but it always made me laugh that is was called Better Than "You Know What Cake" TWO....I guess it stands to reason there is a recipe floating around out there for Better Than "You Know What Cake" ONE! Apparently, since there is now a TWO, the first one wasn't REALLY better then "You Know What." Now, I'm not gonna make any claims about the TWO version, but women to women, the girls and I think if the name isn't true, it's pretty darn close!

- 18.5 oz. German chocolate cake mix
- 1 cup semi-sweet chocolate chips
- 14 oz. can of sweetened condensed milk
- ½ cup caramel sundae topping
- 12 ounce carton frozen whipped topping, thawed
- 3 Heath Bars, crushed

1. Heat oven to 350.
2. Grease and flour a 9 x 13 pan.
3. Prepare cake mix as directed on package and pour into prepared pan.
4. After 10 minutes of baking, remove cake from oven and sprinkle with chocolate chips.
5. Return to oven and continue baking until cake is done.
6. While cake is still hot, use the end of a wooden spoon to poke several holes in the top of the cake.
7. Pour sweetened condensed milk over the cake.
8. Let cake cool completely.
9. Top with caramel sauce, then whipped topping.
10. Sprinkle with candy pieces.

Keep cake refrigerated. It gets better the next day! Enjoy.

Serves 12-15

a quick POINT

Our Favorite Store-Bought Desserts:

Denise: Costco's 7 lb. chocolate cake. It's beautiful and is still super moist and delicious.

Leigh: Mine would be Mayfield Moose Tracks Ice Cream, frozen Snicker bars and Chocolate Honey Dipped Dunkin Donuts.

Shelley: Hands down, my all time favorite dessert has ALWAYS been a really great sugar cookie with butter cream icing. POG's favorite in all the world

happen to come from a line of stores that started in Indiana called Blondie's Cookies. We send these for Christmas gifts every year and people can't WAIT to get them. Do yourself, and everyone you know, a favor; order some NOW!! They are the best cookies you will ever put in your mouth. Their website is www.blondiescookies.com. Tell them Point of Grace sent you! As for other desserts, I truly believe, unless you're willing to pay BIG BUCKS, that no one makes a better, more reasonably priced birthday cake than Sam's Club Bakery. Call me crazy, but their white cake with butter cream icing is my all time favorite.

MIRIAM'S PUMPKIN PIE

from DENISE

As picky as my husband is, the last thing I would have ever guessed that he would like is pumpkin pie. So, on the first Thanksgiving we shared together I about fell out of my chair when I saw him eat a slice. It was my grandmother's special recipe, so I made sure that she passed it along to me. When it came time for me to make Thanksgiving dinner in Tennessee, I made it for him. I didn't attempt a turkey or homemade stuffing, but I was able to accomplish this pie fairly well. There is something special about this particular recipe that puts it ahead of other pumpkin pie recipes, in my opinion!

- 9-inch pie shell (frozen)
- 1 T. Knox gelatin
- 1½ cups pumpkin
- 1 cup sugar
- ½ cup milk
- ¼ t. ginger
- 2 t. cinnamon
- ¼ t. salt
- ¼ t. allspice
- 2 T. margarine or butter
- 3 eggs

1. Bake a pie shell in a 9-inch pie pan.
2. Mix gelatin and ¼ cup water and set aside.
3. Put everything in double boiler except eggs and gelatin.
4. Beat egg yolks, add to mixture, mix until thick.
5. Add gelatin and stir 'til dissolved, then let double boiler cool. (You might even want to put in fridge while doing step 6.)
6. Beat 3 egg whites and 2 t. sugar 'til whites are stiff.
7. Mix with pumpkin mixture and pour into the already cooked pie shell.
8. Refrigerate at least 4 hours. I like to serve it with whipped cream.

Serves 8

DAISY'S VANILLA TAFFY

from DENISE

Making this vanilla taffy with my grandmother Daisy is such a fun Christmas memory I have. She loved candy and I must have gotten that gene from her because I love it too! This particular candy is not as fun to do without a partner because you have to pull the taffy yourself. So, every Christmas my 3 sisters, my mom, and my grandmother would get together for a candy making night. Most of the time it consisted of cinnamon and peppermint hard candy, popcorn balls and Vanilla Taffy. I hope you can take some time to do this with your kids or grandkids. It not only tastes good, but it is fun to do, as well!

- 1 cup sugar
- ⅔ cup light corn syrup
- ½ cup water
- ¼ t. cream of tartar
- 1 t. vanilla
- 1 T. butter or margarine

1. Butter a large platter or jellyroll pan
2. Combine sugar, corn syrup, water and cream of tartar in medium-size heavy saucepan. Bring to a boil over medium heat, stirring constantly.
3. Boil mixture, without stirring, until the candy thermometer, if you have one, registers 266 degrees. (A teaspoon of the mixture will form a hard ball when dropped in cold water if it is done.)
4. Remove from heat; stir in vanilla and butter.
5. Pour onto prepared platter or jelly-roll pan. Let candy stand until cool enough to handle.
6. Wash and dry your hands really well then put butter on them.
7. Gather up candy; pull between your hands until it becomes satiny and light in color.
8. Pull into long strips; twist.
9. Cut into 1-inch pieces with scissors. To store, wrap and place in an airtight container.

Makes ½ a pound

My mom, my sisters and Daisy

BLUEBERRY BANANA DESSERT

from LEIGH

My dear friend and neighbor Peggy told me about blueberry pickin'. She said the kids would LOVE it and did they ever! One very hot summer we went blueberry pickin' in Franklin, TN. I had no idea how much fun kids would have workin' towards filling up their own bucket and how much I would benefit from all those fresh blueberries. Here is another way we ALL can benefit from Peggy's blueberry wisdom. Thanks Peggy!

- 1 roll of sugar cookie dough
- 2 or 3 bananas
- 8 oz. cream cheese, softened
- 15 oz. sweetened condensed milk
- 1 t. vanilla
- ⅓ cup lemon juice
- 1½ cups fresh blueberries

First Layer (crust):
1. Cut roll of sugar cookie dough into quarter inch slices.
2. Place slices to cover bottom and sides of 13x9 pan that has been sprayed with cooking spray.
3. Bake until light brown. Cool. (You can also use a graham cracker crust.)

Second Layer:
4. Slice bananas and cover the cool crust.

Third Layer (filling):
4. Beat softened cream cheese until fluffy.
5. Gradually add condensed milk, stirring constantly. Stir until thoroughly mixed.
6. Add lemon juice and vanilla. Mix well.
7. Spread evenly on top of bananas.
8. Chill until firm. Then add top layer.

Top Layer:
9. Spread blueberries on top.
10. Return to refrigerator. (Total chill time at least 3 hours before serving.)

Serves 10-12

We had a "berry" good time pickin' blueberries!

CHAPTER NINE

SO, BREAKFAST
IS NOT JUST FOR BREAKFAST ANYMORE

Technically, these recipes are all breakfast food. However, if you are like us and love muffins for dessert, sausage for dinner and coffee cake for a midnight snack, then this chapter is for you! And oh yeah, these work really well for breakfast, too!

SAUSAGE STREUDEL

from SHELLEY

I remember the first time I ever tasted this recipe. It was Christmas morning a few years ago and my husband David, my daughter Caroline and I were spending Christmas with my family in Little Rock. My mom pulled this yummy smelling "hot sausage bread thing" out of the oven and I fell in love with it. It's different than the same ol' breakfast fare, but very tasty and easy to make. Serve it with a simple fruit salad and you have a great breakfast that is just a little special and out of the ordinary.

- 1 lb. hot pork sausage
- 2 eggs
- ¾ cup parmesan cheese
- 1 T. melted butter, plus a little extra for spreading on top!
- 1 roll of frozen bread dough, thawed
- dash of paprika

1. Preheat oven to 350.
2. Pan-fry the sausage until done, breaking into small bits.
3. Pour off grease and let cool.
4. Add eggs, parmesan cheese and 1 T. of the melted butter to the sausage.
5. Set aside.
6. Roll out bread dough and place on a greased baking sheet.
7. Spread sausage mixture evenly on dough.
8. Roll up lengthwise. Pinch seams and fold ends.
9. Lay the filled bread dough on its seam on a greased baking sheet. Butter the top generously and sprinkle with paprika.
10. Bake for 35 minutes. Slice and serve hot.

The finished sausage streudel

Serves 8-10

EGGS "BENNIE"

from LEIGH

This is my new favorite breakfast recipe. It makes me feel like a real cook. I was in my early 30's when I tasted Eggs Benedict for the first time. I absolutely loved how all of the ingredients mixed together in my mouth. It was love at first bite! (It may have had something to do with the location. I was in Maui, out on the terrace overlooking the ocean!) Since then I always order it when given the opportunity. I never considered making it myself until I saw just how easy it was! Trust me, if I can do it, ANYONE can.

- non-stick cooking spray
- 12 eggs
- 12 slices Canadian bacon
- 6 English muffins, spilt (I prefer wheat)
- 6 tablespoons butter, softened
- Bennie sauce (recipe below)
- snipped chives, for garnish (I don't usually have this)
- silicone muffin trays (mine are red and were worth getting at Bed, Bath and Beyond)

Bennie sauce:
- ½ cup Duke's mayonnaise
- 2 T. Dijon mustard
- 1 t. cayenne pepper
- 1 t. lemon juice, freshly squeezed

1. Preheat oven to 375.
2. Combine all sauce ingredients in a bowl and mix well.
3. Put two 6-cup silicone muffin trays on a baking sheet, and coat well with non-stick spray. Crack an egg into each muffin cup.
4. Cover each egg with a slice of Canadian bacon.
5. Butter the English muffins and place them butter side down on top of the Canadian bacon.
6. Bake for 15 minutes.
7. Remove from the oven and let rest for 5 minutes.
8. Cover the muffin pan with a platter; flip over.
9. Squeeze each of the muffin cups to release the eggs, then carefully remove.
10. Top each egg with a spoonful of Bennie sauce.
11. Sprinkle with chives (if you have them).

(Just fyi, the first time my mom and I made this, we did not put enough non-stick spray in each cup. Do a "gracious plenty" in order for the "flip over" to not be a "flop out.")

Serves 12

BREAKFAST CASSEROLE

from LEIGH

When we have guests stay overnight at the Cappillino "B & B," we always offer this breakfast casserole. The main reason is that I can prepare it the night before. This allows me to get up quietly and put it in the oven without disturbing sleeping guests. They awaken to the smell of coffee brewing and sausage cooking. They can't help but feel a warm fuzzy of comfort. I will often add a fruit tray (whatever is in season) because this is my favorite taste combination: sweet (the fruit) and savory (the casserole). Good morning!

- 6 slices white bread
- 1 pound mild sausage
- 6 eggs
- 12 oz. sharp cheddar cheese, grated
- 2 cups half & half
- ½ t. salt
- ½ t. pepper
- 1 t. dry mustard

1. Trim crusts from bread.
2. Butter bread and cut into fourths.
3. Line bottom of 9x13 dish with bread.
4. Brown sausage and drain well.
5. Sprinkle sausage over bread.
6. Top with cheese.
7. Beat eggs and add remaining ingredients.
8. Cover and chill for 8 hours or overnight.
9. Bake for 20-25 minutes on 350 – starting in cold oven (not preheated).

Serves 10-12

a quick POINT

So, Here's Who Taught Me To Cook:

My foundation of cooking basics came from **my mom** but I also tip my "pan" to other family members. **My granddaddy**'s (Mom's side) strong influence is in many of my recipes and my **Granny Darby** (Dad's side) influenced the messy cook in me. (Her biscuits were delicious but her kitchen was engulfed in flour during the process!) **Daddy** was a

LEIGH

tremendous influence too. I began working as a waitress when I was 17 in his first restaurant, "Bob's Country Kitchen" (home of the BEST chili cheeseburger). **Aunt Dot** was a waitress and cook and I watched her put the "goodness" on very simple dishes. (I call it "country -fied.") My **Aunt Billie Jo** taught me only ONE dish but this dish wins rave reviews everywhere I go. You can try her Mackie Pie yourself. (See Side Dishes.) I conclude with the influence of my cohorts. Believe it or not, I have called on Shelley and Denise many times over the years!

SAUSAGE & CRISP RICE CASSEROLE

from DENISE

This recipe reminds me of my Baptist church and all of the wonderful ladies who would cook for everything. For my birthday every year, I always asked for sausage casserole for breakfast. I could've eaten the entire pan if I was allowed to!

- 4 cups of crisp rice cereal
- 2 lbs. sausage meat (browned and drained)
- 1 medium onion (chopped and browned)
- 1 stick Cracker Barrel sharp cheddar cheese (grated)
- 1½ cups cooked rice
- 4 eggs
- 2 cans cream of celery soup

1. Preheat oven to 325.
2. In a 9x13 casserole dish, layer cereal, sausage, onion, rice and cheese.
3. Pour mixture of beaten eggs and celery soup over the rest of ingredients.
4. Sprinkle cereal over the top.
5. Bake for 45 minutes.

a quick POINT

So, Here's Who Taught Me To Cook:

Who says that I know how to cook? (Ha ha!) We had talked about having a "So you think you can't cook" chapter in our cookbook and I'm pretty sure that's where most of my recipes would have ended up! From time to time I observed **my grandmothers** and **my mom** while they were cooking. However, I tended to be out in the driveway shooting hoops, so I really wasn't in the kitchen all that much. These days, I don't live close enough to Mom to get many cooking tips, therefore, **Shelley** and my friend **Karri** end up answering most of my cooking questions.

DENISE

Serve with fresh fruit and sweet rolls. Freezes well. (To extend the recipe to two casserole dishes, add 2 more eggs.)

Serves 10-12

GREEN CHILE FRITTATA

from SHELLEY

I know you're probably thinking, "How can something with only three ingredients really be 'cookbook worthy'?" Whip up this dish for breakfast and you will soon find out! I love things that you can make the night before and just pop in the oven the next morning. This fits the bill and is a great option for a brunch when you want something special with just a little "kick!" (Thanks to Julie's Aunt Margaret in Lampasas, TX for this one!)

- 3 cans whole green chiles
- 12 to 16 oz. shredded Monterey Jack cheese
- 4 eggs, beaten

1. Split chiles open, remove seeds and rinse.
2. Dry with paper towels.
3. Line pie plate with chiles, skin side down.
4. Put cheese on top of chiles.
5. Pour beaten eggs over cheese.
6. Refrigerate overnight.
7. Put in cold oven and bake at 325 for 25-30 minutes, until set.

Serves 6-8

a quick POINT

So, Here's Who Taught Me To Cook:

SHELLEY

My mother was a big influence in my life as far as cooking goes. I wouldn't say that I was too interested in it growing up, but I think you learn some things simply by osmosis! She would try to get us to help her, and on the rare occasion we actually would. But most of the time we couldn't be bothered. I think something clicked for me when I got married. There was something about getting all those new dishes that just made me want to actually use my kitchen. I love having people over now and I call my mom ALL the time with questions about cooking and recipes. It's almost like she is the "cooking hotline" or something. There are many times I would have been in trouble if not for good ol' Mom on the other end of the line.

TERRI'S BAKED OATMEAL

from DENISE

So, I never was a big fan of oatmeal for breakfast, until we went to our mentor, Terri's house for a meeting one morning. She greeted us with a warm hug and a table set with Baked Oatmeal and I immediately changed my mind. I DO like oatmeal!

- ½ cup butter, melted
- 1 cup brown sugar
- 2 eggs, beaten
- 2 T. milk
- 3 cups old fashioned oatmeal
- 2½ t. baking powder
- 1 t. salt
- 1 cup milk

1. Preheat oven to 350.
2. Combine and mix first 4 ingredients.
3. Add remaining ingredients and mix.
4. Put in greased 9x9 pan.
5. Bake for 40-60 min.

Serve warm with milk and fresh fruit.

Serves 6-8
(double to fit 9x13 recipe)

Terri and POG, with the baked oatmeal!

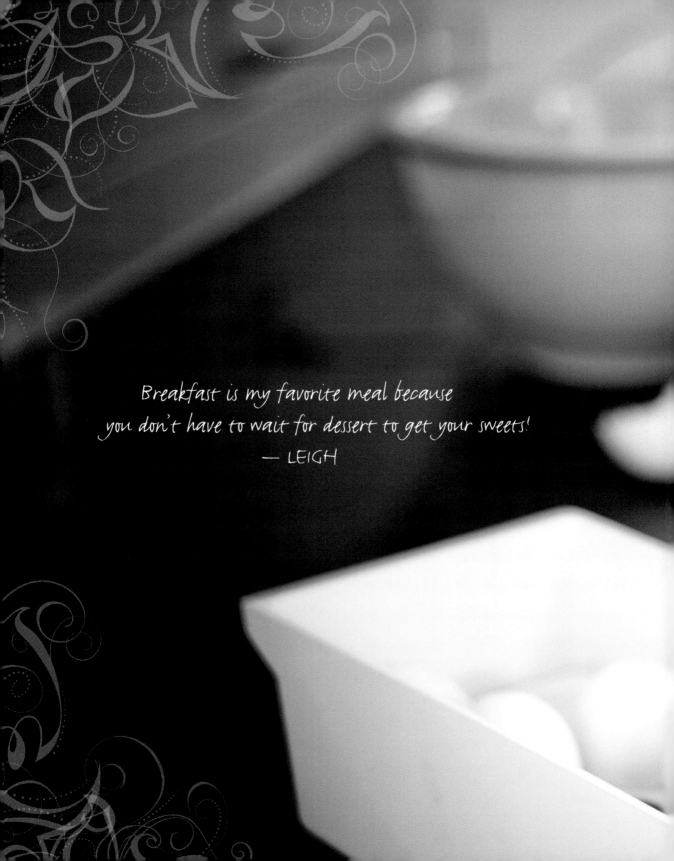

*Breakfast is my favorite meal because
you don't have to wait for dessert to get your sweets!*
— LEIGH

BREAKFAST PASTA SKILLET

from LEIGH

We all have people in our lives who cheer us on and encourage us. This recipe comes from one of those people in POG's life, Gator Michaels. What was, in the beginning, a business relationship, is now a friendship for a lifetime. Gator helped us during a stressful time of transition. He encouraged us to keep our focus and stay the course. Gator brings warmth to a room and his kindness towards others is one of his greatest qualities. He often speaks of his grandmother (and if I am not mistaken this awesome recipe can be traced back to her), so when he told me about Breakfast Pasta he had my undivided attention.

- 2 cups penne or farfalle pasta
- 3 large eggs
- 1 clove minced garlic
- 2 T. olive oil
- ½ t. red pepper
- ¾ t. onion powder
- ¾ t. dried parsley
- ¾ t. basil
- ¾ t. oregano leaves
- pinch of salt
- ¼ cup grated parmesan cheese
- ¼ grated romano cheese

Gator... His smile says it all... he is the nicest!

1. Cook pasta as directed.
2. In a large skillet sauté garlic in olive oil for 5 minutes over medium heat.
3. In a medium bowl mix eggs and the rest of the spices.
4. As soon as the pasta is cooked drain without rinsing, add to skillet and stir.
5. Stir in eggs and spices.
6. Stir in cheese.

That's it. The eggs will cook very quickly, so once you mix in the cheese it's ready for the table.

Serves 2-3

GARLIC & CHEESE GRITS

from SHELLEY

I have honestly never been much of a grits lover. Weird, I know, being from Arkansas and all, but my mom just never made them. I remember my Grandma Ruby who lived in Tennessee making them every once in a while, but I always thought they looked gross and would never try them. Enter Cracker Barrel. I finally tried grits there a few years ago and I loved them! I believe they were some kind of cheese grits. I'm still not real big on plain ol'grits, but add a little cheese and garlic and bam! So good! You will love these grits, even if you don't love grits. I speak from experience.

- 1 cup grits (quick grits, not instant)
- 6 oz. roll garlic cheese (usually available for Christmas season, if not available, substitute 6 oz. American cheese and ½ t. garlic powder)
- 2 eggs
- half & half
- ½ stick butter

1. Pre-heat oven to 375.
2. Cook grits according to package directions.
3. Add cheese and butter and mix well.
4. Beat eggs in 1 cup measuring cup.
5. With eggs still in cup, fill the rest of the way with half & half.
6. Add to grits and mix well.
7. Pour into greased, 2 quart casserole dish.
8. Bake 25 minutes or until set.

Serves 6-8

STUFFED FRENCH TOAST

from LEIGH

This is the perfect dish for kids. Something sweet for them and something easy for Mom. I love that you can prepare it the night before. Perfect for a relaxing morning with family over juice and coffee.

- 8 slices of bread (3 or 4 day old bread is best)
- 12 eggs
- ⅓ cup maple syrup
- 1 cup milk
- 1 cup half & half
- 16 oz. cream cheese
- 1 t. vanilla
- ¼ t. nutmeg

1. Remove crusts from bread and cube it.
2. Place half in bottom of 9x13 pan.
3. Cube cream cheese and place on top of bread in pan.
4. Put remaining bread on top of the cream cheese.
5. Break the eggs and combine with the maple syrup, milk and half & half.
6. Pour over the bread mixture.
7. Cover with plastic wrap and place in refrigerator overnight.
8. Bake at 375 for 45 minutes or until done.
9. Remove from oven and sprinkle cinnamon on top.

Serve with syrup or fruit.

Serves 8-10

COOKING CLASS #9

BE FRUITFUL How to make beautiful fruit arrangements:
On several of these breakfast recipes we have suggested that you serve fruit as a side dish. Here are some ways to make the presentation of the fruit beautiful:

1. **Fruit Skewers** – arrange whole strawberries, green grapes, fresh pineapple chunks, red grapes and blueberries on a wooden skewer. You can do a pattern or just slide fruit on skewer at random. On some skewers put only strawberries or only blueberries, etc. to change it up a little bit. When you have made about 10-12 skewers (or enough to feed your family), place them in a pretty pitcher or vase.

2. **Melon Ball Fruit Salad** – using a rounded teaspoon (if your measuring spoons are round you won't need to go buy a special utensil) make a deep scoop into melon using a circular motion to round all sides, forming a ball. Repeat this process using watermelon, honey dew and cantaloupe. You can also use smaller or larger rounded spoons to make a variety of sizes. Serve in a pretty glass bowl.

3. **Rainbow Fruit Platter** – on a round platter arrange bands of fruit in rings starting with the outer edge and ending in the middle of tray. Example – the first ring is red grapes – line them all the way around edge of tray; the next ring is pineapple chunks followed by strawberries and so forth. You can make a pretty flower design in the middle using a strawberry as the center and green grapes (or peach slices) as "petals."

BROWN SUGAR
& PECAN COFFEE CAKE

from DENISE

Everyone needs a good, basic coffee cake recipe to pull out for a last minute occasion. This one is quick and easy, making it perfect for all types of events: Bible studies, dessert, brunch, or afternoon tea. There is never any left on the serving plate!

Cake:
- ¼ cup oil
- 1 egg, beaten
- ½ cup milk
- 1½ cup flour
- ¾ cup sugar
- 2 t. baking powder
- ½ t. salt

Topping:
- ¼ cup brown sugar
- 1 T. flour
- 1 t. cinnamon
- 1 T. melted butter
- ½ cup chopped pecans

1. Preheat oven to 375.
2. Combine oil, egg and milk, mix well.
3. Add flour, sugar, baking powder and salt.
4. Pour into greased, square baking pan.
5. Combine topping ingredients and sprinkle on top.
6. Bake for 25 minutes or until light brown.

Serves 6-8

Variation - this cake works great for strawberry shortcake. Instead of the brown sugar topping above, heap fresh strawberries on top and cover with whipped cream! Perfect on a hot summer day. YUM!

menu SUGGESTIONS

BABY SHOWER BRUNCH
Breakfast Casserole, Sausage Streudel, Garlic/Cheese Grits, Pumpkin/Chocolate Chip Muffins and orange/cranberry juice (mix 1 part orange juice with 1 part cranberry juice and serve from clear, glass pitcher)

CONTINENTAL SPREAD
Overnight Pull-Aparts, Baked Oatmeal, Brown Sugar & Pecan Coffee Cake and Fruit Skewers (from Cooking Class)

HEARTY BREAKFAST
Stuffed French Toast, Green Chile Frittata, Garlic/Cheese Grits, Bacon and store-bought biscuits (the biscuit dough from the freezer section that comes in a bag is best)

OVERNIGHT PULL-APARTS

from DENISE

As a mom, I love the wonderful opportunity to see Christmas through the eyes of my children. However, no matter how organized I am (or am not), I am exhausted Christmas morning. Staying up 'til the early hours of the morning wrapping gifts or helping Santa by putting a toy together leaves the morning with the need for A LOT of coffee! My boys always wake up super early, ready to go! After they have looked in their stockings and played with some of the new toys, they are ready to eat. Pull-Aparts are the perfect Christmas morning bread. While you are up wrapping presents the night before, you put the ingredients in the pan. Then all you have to do Christmas morning is preheat the oven, bake and "Ta Da" - they are ready to go! Plus they are really pretty to set out with your Christmas dishes.

- 24 frozen (unraised) parker house rolls
- ½ cup sugar
- ½ cup brown sugar
- 1 T. cinnamon
- 1 package (3 5/8 oz.) butterscotch pudding mix - not instant
- 1 stick butter, melted

1. Grease bundt pan and place frozen rolls in it.
2. Mix all ingredients except butter and sprinkle over rolls.
3. Pour butter over the top.
4. Let sit overnight.
5. In the morning, preheat oven to 350 and bake for 30 minutes.
6. Let stand 5-10 minutes before inverting to plate.

Serves 10-12

We made this for Christmas 2009

PUMPKIN/CHOCOLATE CHIP MUFFINS

from SHELLEY

I referred to these muffins that my neighbor Kathy makes in our appetizer chapter. These are the "I'm sorry my dog stole your child's stuffed animal" muffins that I found in my mailbox. I have been in love with them ever since. I know it's fall when somehow or another I get some of Kathy Z.'s little mini pumpkin muffins. They are perfect for breakfast or even a little afternoon snack. They are moist, a little bit sweet and just delicious! Make some for your friends and an extra batch just for you!

- 1⅔ cups flour
- ¾ cup sugar
- 1 T. pumpkin pie spice
- 1 t. baking soda
- ¼ t. baking powder
- ¼ t. salt
- 2 eggs, beaten
- ½ cup butter, melted
- 1 cup canned pumpkin
- 1 cup semi-sweet chocolate chips

1. Preheat oven to 350.
2. Mix flour, sugar, pumpkin pie spice, soda, baking powder, and salt together in a separate bowl.
3. Combine butter, eggs, and pumpkin. Mix well.
4. Stir in chocolate chips.
5. Pour this mixture over dry ingredients, then fold together.
6. Fill muffin cups half full.
7. Bake 12-15 minutes for mini muffin pans, 20-25 minutes for regular size muffin pans.

Makes 4 dozen mini muffins or 2 dozen regular size muffins

SCRAMBLED EGGS & RED PEPPERS ON FRENCH BREAD TOAST

from SHELLEY

If I can't live in Arkansas, then Tennesse is the next best thing! People often refer to Nashville as a "little big town," and it's true. There's lots to do in the way of arts and entertainment, but it feels like a small town because everyone is so connected. This is especially true in the music community. I got to meet Suzy Bogguss, one of the great voices of country music, many years ago through a mutual friend, and I always enjoy getting to see her. She is an excellent cook, and said she hopes to write a cookbook one day, too! I will be the first in line to buy it! She was so sweet to contribute this original breakfast recipe that her family enjoys ...

- 4 large eggs
- 4 large egg whites
- ¼ cup skim or 2% milk
- ½ t. salt and more to taste
- ¼ t. freshly ground black pepper
- 2 t. olive oil
- 1 garlic clove (finely chopped)
- 1 small jar roasted red peppers (drained, rinsed and coarsely chopped)
- ¼ t. dried, rubbed sage
- 4-6 pieces crusty French or Italian bread
- 8 black or green olives pitted and minced (Take the blade of a large kitchen knife and smash the olives on a cutting board, rubbing the knife flat to almost make a paste - like tapenade.)

A NOTE FROM
SUZY BOGGUSS

I discovered this recipe one winter when we were actually snowbound in Nashville. I had to make due with my gas stove for cooking and for heat. I also had to make do with what was available in the fridge. It has become a weekend favorite at our house. You can round the meal out with bacon and/or fruit but little ol' us had to make due with Kool-Aid!

1. Whisk the eggs, including the extra whites, with milk, salt and pepper; set aside.
2. Heat the oil in a large nonstick skillet over low heat. Add the garlic and cook for 2 minutes being careful that it just goes to light brown.
3. Pour the egg mixture into the skillet and cook the eggs until they are holding together in creamy clumps.
4. Remove from the heat and stir in the red peppers and sage. Check to see if they need more salt and pepper.
5. Toast the bread (you may use baguette if you like a smaller piece) and spread with the olive paste. Spoon the eggs on top of the toast and gobble them up!

Keely Scott, John Grimes, Shelley, Jill Tomalty and Suzy Bogguss

Serves 4

DARBY'S DELIGHTFUL SURPRISE

from LEIGH

Now this is the name my daughter Darby gave this recipe. She and I just decided to raid the refrigerator one morning and this is what we came up with. I'll have you know, it has now become quite the staple in our home for breakfast, especially in the summer. Have fun with the kids on this one.

- 32 oz. vanilla yogurt
- ½ cup of half & half
- 1 cup strawberries
- 1 cup blueberries
- 1 banana (or 2 for thicker texture)
- ½ cup orange juice
- 1 t. of cinnamon
  (Darby considers this the SECRET ingredient)

1. Get your favorite blender down and combine all ingredients in it.
2. Mix until well blended.
3. Add a few ice cubes and continue to blend.
4. Keep adding ice cubes until it reaches desired consistency.
5. Pour into a pretty glass and garnish with a mint leaf.

Makes 4 smoothies

My beautiful daughter Darby

To our readers:

This cookbook was created in part to raise awareness and funds for an organization close to the heart of Point of Grace. A portion of the profits from the sale of this cookbook will go to benefit The Raining Season.

The Raining Season is a Christian based non-profit organization whose mission is to provide a hopeful future to orphaned children and impoverished families in Sierra Leone, West Africa through meeting basic necessities that include: Housing, Nourishment, Education and Small Business Grants.

You may wonder, "Why the name?" It's very simple really. Sierra Leone has two seasons, one is rainy, one is dry. We found that the rainy season is a constant struggle for the people of Sierra Leone. Roads are impassable, labor jobs are difficult to find, and disease is rampant due to the stagnant waters. Maleria and Typhoid fever deaths are at their highest peak during this difficult time of year. It is the goal of all who support this cause to "Help Hope Rain Down" on the children and families that deserve a chance to reach their dreams. This gives profound meaning to the name "The Raining Season."

To make a donation for the children of this organization visit us on the web at www.therainingseason.org.

Thank you in advance for your prayers and support for The Raining Season.

Point of Grace